The Nonprofit
POLICY
SAMPLER

Second Edition

Building Effective Nonprofit Boards

by
Barbara Lawrence
and Outi Flynn

Library of Congress Cataloging-in-Publication Data

Lawrence, Barbara, 1944-

    The nonprofit policy sampler / by Barbara Lawrence and Outi Flynn. – 2nd ed.

    p. cm.

    Rev. ed. of: The policy sampler : a resource for nonprofit boards : user's guide / by Kathleen Fletcher. Washington, DC : National Center for Nonprofit Boards, 2000.

    ISBN 1-58686-034-8 (pbk.)

    1. Directors of corporations – Handbooks, manuals, etc. 2. Nonprofit organizations – Management – Handbooks, manuals, etc. I. Flynn, Outi. II. Fletcher, Kathleen. Policy sampler. III. Title.

HD2745.L32 2006
658.4'22 – dc22

2006026847

© 2006 BoardSource.
First printing, September 2006.
ISBN 1-58686-034-8

Published by BoardSource
1828 L Street, NW, Suite 900
Washington, DC 20036

Formerly the National Center for Nonprofit Boards

BoardSource, formerly the National Center for Nonprofit Boards, is the premier resource for practical information, tools and best practices, training, and leadership development for board members of nonprofit organizations worldwide. Through our highly acclaimed programs and services, BoardSource enables organizations to fulfill their missions by helping build strong and effective nonprofit boards.

BoardSource provides assistance and resources to nonprofit leaders through workshops, training, and our extensive Web site, www.boardsource.org. A team of BoardSource governance consultants works directly with nonprofit leaders to design specialized solutions to meet organizations' needs and assists nongovernmental organizations around the world through partnerships and capacity building. As the world's largest, most comprehensive publisher of materials on nonprofit governance, BoardSource offers a wide selection of books, videotapes, CDs, and online tools. BoardSource also hosts the BoardSource Leadership Forum, bringing together governance experts, board members, and chief executives of nonprofit organizations from around the world.

Created out of the nonprofit sector's critical need for governance guidance and expertise, BoardSource is a 501(c)(3) nonprofit organization that has provided practical solutions to nonprofit organizations of all sizes in diverse communities. In 2001, BoardSource changed its name from the National Center for Nonprofit Boards to better reflect its mission. Today, BoardSource has approximately 11,000 members and has served more than 75,000 nonprofit leaders.

For more information, please visit our Web site, www.boardsource.org, e-mail us at mail@boardsource.org, or call us at 800-883-6262.

Have You Used These BoardSource Resources?

VIDEOS

Meeting the Challenge: An Orientation to Nonprofit Board Service
Speaking of Money: A Guide to Fundraising for Nonprofit Board Members

BOOKS

The Board Chair Handbook
Managing Conflicts of Interest: A Primer for Nonprofit Boards
Driving Strategic Planning: A Nonprofit Executive's Guide
The Board-Savvy CEO: How To Build a Strong, Positive Relationship with Your Board
Presenting: Board Orientation
Presenting: Nonprofit Financials
Meet Smarter: A Guide to Better Nonprofit Board Meetings
The Board Building Cycle: Nine Steps to Finding, Recruiting, and Engaging Nonprofit Board Members
To Go Forward, Retreat! The Board Retreat Handbook
Nonprofit Board Answer Book: Practical Guide for Board Members and Chief Executives
Nonprofit Board Answer Book II: Beyond the Basics
The Nonprofit Legal Landscape
Self-Assessment for Nonprofit Governing Boards
Assessment of the Chief Executive
Fearless Fundraising
The Nonprofit Board's Guide to Bylaws
Understanding Nonprofit Financial Statements
Transforming Board Structure: New Possibilities for Committees and Task Forces

THE GOVERNANCE SERIES

1. *Ten Basic Responsibilities of Nonprofit Boards*
2. *Financial Responsibilities of Nonprofit Boards*
3. *Structures and Practices of Nonprofit Boards*
4. *Fundraising Responsibilities of Nonprofit Boards*
5. *Legal Responsibilities of Nonprofit Boards*
6. *The Nonprofit Board's Role in Setting and Advancing the Mission*
7. *The Nonprofit Board's Role in Planning and Evaluation*
8. *How To Help Your Board Govern More and Manage Less*
9. *Leadership Roles in Nonprofit Governance*

For an up-to-date list of publications and information about current prices, membership, and other services, please call BoardSource at 800-883-6262 or visit our Web site at www.boardsource.org.

Contents

Acknowledgements

No book is ever published without the support of colleagues and friends. But, *The Nonprofit Policy Sampler* is no ordinary book. From nonprofit leaders and for nonprofit leaders, it is a unique compilation of business documents from more than 50 organizations around the country. Without their hard work in developing these documents and generosity of spirit in sharing them, we could not have created this collection. To maintain confidentiality, we have removed all references to individual organizations in these samples, with the exception of the United Way of the National Capital Area (because it is important to understand the circumstances under which it was developed). On behalf of the sector, we would like to name and thank the following contributing organizations:

Alice Paul Institute
Alliance for Continuing Medical Education
American Bar Association
American Cancer Society
American Network of Community Options and Resources
Arcus Foundation
Association for Library Collections & Technical Services
Association for Supervision and Curriculum Development
Bodanna
Center for Science in the Public Interest
Community Foundation of Ottawa
Community Foundation of South Wood County
Council for Christian Colleges & Universities
Council of New Jersey Grantmakers
Dress for Success
The Erie Community Foundation
The Fund Raising School, The Center on Philanthropy at Indiana University
Girl Scouts of the South Jersey Pines
Granite Falls School District
Gulf Coast Community Foundation of Venice
Joint Council on International Children's Services
Kentucky-Tennessee Society of American Foresters
The Leadership Group
Lincoln Community Foundation
The Lindenberger Group
Loyola University Chicago
Lucile Packard Foundation for Children's Health
Lutheran World Relief
Michael Smith Foundation for Health Research
National Association of Corporate Directors
National Council of Nonprofit Associations
National League for Nursing
National Precast Concrete Association
Non-Profit Works

Northeastern Integrated Pest Management Center
Pickering Public Library
Pinellas County
Porter-Leath Children's Center
Prevent Child Abuse Kentucky
Ridgefield Symphony Orchestra
Society for Clinical Data Management
Special Libraries Association
Texas Nonprofit Management Assistance Network
Trenton Community Music School
United Way of America
United Way of New York City
United Way of the National Capital Area
University of Florida
University of Louisville
University of Puget Sound
University of Texas Health Science Center at Houston
University System of New Hampshire
Verde Valley Alternative Lifestyles Community
Victims Information Bureau of Suffolk
Volunteer Lawyers and Accountants for the Arts
Washington Apple Education Foundation
West Hills Community College District
The William J. and Dorothy K. O'Neill Foundation
Wolftrap Foundation for the Performing Arts
Women in Transition
World Wildlife Fund
Zeta Phi Beta Sorority, Inc.

BoardSource has a longstanding tradition of having its books peer reviewed. Again, because *The Nonprofit Policy Sampler* is no ordinary book, we took extra measures to ensure that our selection of sample documents was of the highest quality. Thanks to the critical eyes, firsthand experience, and thoughtful edits of a team of 21 industry experts, we are able to bring you a well-vetted set of sample policies. (As with any important documents, however, you should have them reviewed and approved by your own professional advisors.) BoardSource owes a tremendous debt of gratitude to the following peer reviewers:

Thomas F. Blaney, O'Connor Davies Munns & Dobbins, LLP
Marc L. Fleischaker, Arent Fox PLLC
John S. Griswold, Jr., Commonfund Institute
Lea Harvey, BoardSource
Bruce R. Hopkins, Polsinelli Shalton Welte Suelthaus PC
Thomas K. Hyatt, Ober|Kaler
M. Elaine Jacoby, Duane Morris, LLP
William F. Jarvis, Commonfund Institute
Jane Kornblut, Third Sector Services, LLC
Bruce Lesley, Nonprofit Strategic Directions
Mark Light, First Light Group LLC

Thomas McLaughlin, Grant Thornton LLP
Terri O'Brien, BoardSource
Patrick O'Hare, Ober|Kaler
Deanne M. Ottaviano, Arent Fox PLLC
Sally J. Patterson, Radiant Communications
Marci Sunderland, BoardSource
Ben Tesdahl, Powers, Pyles, Sutter & Verville
Brian H. Vogel, Quatt Associates
Charles M. (Chip) Watkins, Webster, Chamberlain & Bean
Carol Weisman, Board Builders

Preface

In his book, *Policy Management in the Human Services*, John Tropman defines policy as an idea that is embodied in a written document, is ratified by legitimate authority, and serves as a guide to action. The major policies of a nonprofit organization are created and ratified by its board of directors, are (or should be) written down in a policy manual for easy reference, are (or should be) reviewed frequently to see if they are up to date, and cover every aspect of the organization's business.

While bylaws are the foundation for the organization's structure, policies put meat on the bylaw bones to cover the myriad of situations that are not addressed in the bylaws. Many organizations intentionally make bylaws hard to amend so that fundamental structures cannot be overturned by majority rule. Policies, however, are more flexible so that decision makers can respond to immediate needs and the majority of the board can establish and change policies. Policies are created for programs, financial management, fundraising, personnel management, public relations, and board operations.

Policies are created at different levels and by different individuals or entities depending on their ultimate purpose. The chief executive is responsible for drafting policies to guide operations and manage staff. Financial staff ensures that proper policies are in place to guide accounting practices and investment management. The board establishes policies to coordinate its own affairs and its oversight of the organization. Even if it is not directly involved in drafting the actual policies, the board must ensure that policies exist, comply with the law, cover critical issues, and remain current. Because the board has ultimate responsibility and accountability for the organization, it needs to ensure that organizational policies at all levels are well documented and routinely followed.

The Nonprofit Policy Sampler is designed to help nonprofit leaders — board and staff — advance their organizations, make better collective decisions, and guide individual actions and behaviors. It contains sample policies, codes, committee charters, job descriptions, and other statements that will help boards move forward in the essential governance task of policy-making. Divided into eight broad categories, it contains 241 electronic samples addressing 48 different issues. Each policy issue includes key elements, practical tips, samples, and additional resources on the subject. *The Nonprofit Policy Sampler* — available in print with a companion CD-ROM and online in downloadable format — offers an array of different approaches for each organization to use as a starting point in developing its own policies.

The Nonprofit Policy Sampler, *its companion CD-ROM, and the downloadable files are intended for educational and informational purposes only. Nothing contained in them is to be construed as the rendering of legal, financial, or other professional advice for specific cases. Readers are responsible for obtaining such advice from their own professional counsel.*

Introduction

Policies are written rules, statements, principles, or directives for making decisions and taking action. Their purpose is to serve as a guide when the board carries out its governance duties and while staff conducts the organization's daily operations. Policies also establish a standard and recommended way of acting in challenging situations. They function as a protective mechanism for the organization and for individuals when a decision is questioned; those responsible can explain how they reached their conclusion by pointing to an approved policy that was followed.

For nonprofit organizations, policies are tools for setting priorities, making decisions, and defining and delegating responsibilities. Too often, policies are created to be sure a bad decision made during a crisis is never repeated. But, policy-making need not be reactive. In fact, it is far more effective when done proactively. It often begins with the need to address situations that are common to all organizations, such as conflicts of interest. It is also done preemptively to handle situations that are anticipated as part of a significant organizational change (such as starting an endowment) or opportunities that emerge over time (such as sponsorship). Boards that practice proactive policy-making can save themselves a great deal of anguish in a crisis situation that demands an immediate response.

CORE ORGANIZATIONAL DOCUMENTS

Policies are part of the core organizational documents that reflect how a nonprofit fulfills its mission and carries out its business in an orderly, legal manner. Defining policy and its place in an organization's structure is not always easy. In practice, it falls into a hierarchy of rules that flow from government regulation and other compliance requirements. The following structure is one way of understanding how policies relate to an organization's other operating guidelines:

1. The ***articles of incorporation*** are a legal document that outlines the general purpose and structure of the organization and its intent to operate exclusively with a nonprofit purpose. The articles are filed with the state and federal government (if and) when the nonprofit is incorporated. They usually follow a standard form and contain a minimum of detail because they are cumbersome to change.

2. ***Bylaws*** establish the governance structure of a nonprofit. Following a fairly standard format, they define the duties, authority limits, and principal operating procedures for the board and board members. The highest level board policies are embedded in the bylaws. Revising bylaws requires following a specific process and, often, approval by the full membership or board. Thus, they too, should not contain overly detailed procedures or restrictions.

3. ***Policies*** come next in the hierarchy. They serve as operating guidelines at various levels. Some policies set out organizational guidelines for board and staff behavior, such as whistleblower protection and gift acceptance policies. Others supplement the bylaws and guide board practices and oversight

procedures, such as investment, internal controls, and executive compensation policies. Still others direct staff operations, such as personnel and communications policies. Many policies not only apply to the work of the staff, but also have implications for the board.

4. A **resolution** is a specific board decision that describes an action to be taken or a principle to be adopted. Resolutions are specific to a particular board for a given situation. They range from broad statements about organizational values (such as protecting the environment) to elevated recognition of significant contributions (of exemplary board members or retiring staff, for example).

5. **Recommendations and guidelines** are often nonbinding but helpful suggestions for actions or behavior. Coming from the board, the language is more suggestive than directive, as it would be for a policy where the statement is clear and resembles an order. For example, after a lengthy discussion, the board might establish criteria to guide the staff in launching a new program; these criteria may not warrant a formal policy or procedure, but will be taken into consideration.

6. **Procedures** define a process for implementing a general policy. There is often a blurry line between policies and procedures because it can be difficult to separate *what* gets done from *how* it gets done. In practice, policies should set the broadest parameters, and procedures should be handled by staff at the implementation level. But, because the process sometimes matters as much as the results — to ensure transparency, participation, and accountability — some procedures are treated more like policies.

A BRIEF OVERVIEW OF POLICY GOVERNANCE®

Determining what issues warrant policy is not easy for nonprofit boards. To help boards understand their roles and responsibilities, especially vis-à-vis professional staff, John Carver introduced Policy Governance® in the late 1970s. His model, presented in the most recent edition of *Boards That Make a Difference* (Jossey-Bass, 2006) treats policies as action plans at the strategic level. It consists of four broad policy areas, within which more specific policies are nested: 1) "Ends" policies are mission related and serve as a long-range plan. 2) "Executive Limitations" policies define boundaries for staff activity. 3) "Board-Executive Linkage" policies clarify the way the board delegates authority to the chief executive and evaluates his or her performance. 4) "Board Process" policies deal with how the board governs itself.

While evidence is equivocal about whether Policy Governance® is more effective than other approaches, research has shown that intentional efforts to improve governance are generally successful. So, what matters is that nonprofit leaders make a concerted effort to develop policies and practices that help the board and, in turn, the organization, to deliver on its mission.

PROPERLY FITTED POLICIES

The types and content of the policies that an organization adopts depend upon its context. Organizational size, complexity, and maturity inevitably shape policies. A smaller, relatively young organization with few staff may operate with simpler policies than those of a more established organization with a large staff and considerable financial resources. Policies should be selected based on what is appropriate for the organization at that particular time in its life. As an organization evolves, the board and staff should review its policies for relevance and update them as necessary.

Policies are also influenced by mission-based practices and community expectations. Museums need to manage their collections, social service agencies need to protect their clients, foundations need to oversee their investment portfolios, and associations need to address industry standards. While the nonprofit sector shares a set of generally accepted policies, each organization also operates within its own realm of practice. Again, the board and staff should ensure that policies are in keeping with the organization's particular circumstances.

Lastly, and importantly, policies may also depend on government regulations, which vary from location to location. Therefore, policies should not be treated as "off the shelf" clothing; each organization needs a tailor to make policies fit its unique situation. Professional advisors — lawyers, accountants, investment managers, and consultants — can be immensely helpful in developing appropriate policies.

POLICY-MAKING

THE PLAYERS

It is a somewhat artificial dichotomy to simply say that boards make policy and staff implements it. Actually, depending upon the nature of the policy, the chief executive or even other staff may develop and implement policy without consulting or notifying the board. Policies established by the staff must support — and not conflict with — organizationwide policies established by the board. However, this does not excuse the board from its responsibility to stay apprised of the organization's policies.

Usually boards are involved in setting the major policies and then delegate the standard operating procedures to staff, except in the area of board-specific policies. In staffed organizations, too much board involvement in establishing standard operating procedures for the staff risks board micromanagement. In all-volunteer organizations, however, the board is likely to be directly involved in defining and implementing all operating policies and procedures for the organization.

The chief executive and board are responsible for establishing policies regarding their governance roles and responsibilities. The macro issues of how the board operates — board size, officer positions, and committee structure — are usually set forth in the bylaws. But many micro areas are not, and should not be, covered in the bylaws, such as board member fundraising requirements and executive compensation. Boards need policies in these and other areas to clarify expectations and establish guidelines for handling the multitude of complicated situations that arise. Despite the considerable involvement of the chief executive, however, the ultimate policy-making responsibility belongs to the board.

THE PROCESS

A few organizations have diligently documented their policies over the years, and the board periodically reviews and updates them as necessary. Many, however, have accumulated policies haphazardly and maintain them in various places. And, alas, when dealing with a difficult issue, some suffer from the absence of policies and create them retroactively. Whatever the situation, the following key elements are part of a thoughtful, comprehensive approach to developing and maintaining organizational policies:

1. **Start with the end — an up-to-date, comprehensive policy manual — in mind.**

   A manual puts all policy documents in one place, in writing. These policies should be shared with new board members during orientation, and board members should be encouraged to reference them appropriately throughout their tenure. For example, the board should establish policies on executive compensation and then review them when it comes time to conduct the chief executive's performance evaluation. Likewise, all board members should sign a conflict-of-interest disclosure statement annually.

2. **Inventory and identify policies.**

   Look first for policies in the organization's bylaws. Among the policies that you may find are mission statements, board officer duties, and committee charters. Extract clauses that are, themselves, policy statements or that relate to policy issues. Then, search board meeting minutes from recent years for explicit policy decisions and examples of decisions that implicitly suggest policy.

3. **Develop an outline of core policies.**

   Identify the main policy areas. The section headings in this book serve as a good starting point. In the end, the policies will cover a core set of issues common to all types of organizations, such as codes of ethics, and some that apply only to certain kinds of nonprofits, such as membership voting for associations and spending policies for foundations.

4. **Draft and discuss policy recommendations.**

   Someone has to take the first steps: collect and draft policies, identify the discussion issues for each policy, and compile the actual policy manual. Often times, this responsibility is delegated to the governance committee or an ad hoc task force. Inevitability, it will require support from staff and professional advisors (e.g., lawyers, investment managers, accountants). No commitment to developing policy is real without a deadline for review and consideration. Allot time at board meetings to discuss and approve one or more policies.

The board should adopt each policy only after appropriate adaptation and thorough discussion. Ask: Does this proposed policy reflect the organization's values, mission, and goals? How often should it be monitored? Board members should define the policy in the organization's context, explore situations where the proposed policy will be used, consider what problems it will head off and what problems it might create, and discuss any concerns.

5. **Finalize and formalize policies.**

   Approaches to policy document formats vary, and a number of formats are incorporated in this sampler. Common components of a policy document include

   Organization name

   Policy number or policy area within hierarchy

   Policy name

   Introduction or statement of purpose

   Policy statement

   Definitions

   Examples

   Assignment of responsibility

   Monitoring and review schedule

   Date approved

   Date last modified

6. **Use the policies.**

   Harder than crafting policies is bringing them to life. They should guide decisions and actions, meaning, they should not gather dust on a bookshelf but be part of the organization's routine operations. They need to be accessible to staff for reference, at committee meetings for direction, and during key board deliberations for guidance.

7. **Review and update policies.**

   Policies may change over time. In fact, if they don't, the board is probably neglecting them. Some changes are minor — fixing a typo or revising a date. Others are major — adopting a new audit policy. Policy review is more than just looking at the words of a document against basic regulatory requirements. More importantly, it ensures that the policy is being followed. Did the board review the chief executive's performance in a timely, thoughtful manner? Did the organization observe the gift acceptance policy with the new donor? To manage the daunting task of regularly reviewing policies, it may help to delegate the actual policy review to an appropriate committee or a special task force and to stagger the review cycles for different policies.

Unfortunately, nonprofit boards often spend precious time handling avoidable crises, micromanaging competent staff, or remaking decisions. In the end, time invested in making policy now frees up future time for the board to engage in work more productively and directly related to the mission. The purpose of policies, and the value of this book, is to help nonprofits improve their governance and thus increase their ability to achieve their mission — to make a difference.

How To Use *The Nonprofit Policy Sampler*

The Nonprofit Policy Sampler is a launch pad for making and revising policies. It contains 241 policies, codes of ethics, mission and vision statements, board member agreements, committee charters, and job descriptions. It is available in print with a companion CD-ROM and online as downloadable files. *The Nonprofit Policy Sampler* is not meant to be an exhaustive source of all organizational or even board policies. Rather, it is intended as a menu of choices to help nonprofit leaders jump-start the essential governance task of policy-making.

BoardSource acknowledges that *The Nonprofit Policy Sampler* is not a complete compendium of organizational or board policies; the samples reflect those most commonly found (and requested) in the nonprofit sector. While the tool includes both governance and operational policies, the emphasis is on issues related to board roles and structure, as well as important organizational matters (e.g., personnel and public relations). Certain other organizational issues, such as program oversight and facilities maintenance, are so specific to individual organizations that they are not included here, although the board should be involved in reviewing and approving such policies.

The introductory text for each category describes the general issues, highlights key elements in understanding the policies, and offers practical tips for creating and implementing the policies. It is followed by brief descriptions of the different samples provided electronically. When drafting or updating policies for your organization, we recommend reviewing all of the samples to better understand the different approaches and nuances of the issue.

BoardSource collected these policies and other documents from organizations of varying size, scope, mission, location, and tax-exempt status. Each of the policies has been edited to eliminate any reference to the organization responsible for its sub-mission. Some policies are brief and general, others provide specific, detailed information. As samples from real organizations, rather than a singular standardized policy, they reveal the range of approaches nonprofit organizations use when setting policy. While *The Nonprofit Policy Sampler* has been vetted by a team of professional advisors and nonprofit practitioners, it is incumbent upon each organization to tailor policies to its own situation and have them reviewed by professional counsel.

Customizing the Electronic Files

While the pages that follow provide an introduction to each policy category, the companion CD-ROM and downloadable files give nonprofit leaders a variety of different sample policies, statements, and job descriptions to choose from and customize. You may adapt these policies freely for your own needs, but the CD-ROM is the copyright of BoardSource and is protected by federal copyright law. **Unauthorized duplication and distribution of these files is in violation of that copyright.** However, as a purchaser of this resource, you are entitled to save this information to your hard drive, or make a backup CD in the event that the original files become corrupted.

The sample documents have been provided in both Microsoft Word (.doc) and plain text (.txt) formats. To customize a policy for a specific organization, simply use the search-and-replace function to replace the letters "XYZ" with the name of your organization.

Throughout this resource, the term "board chair" is used to identify the board's principal leader. Likewise, the term "chief executive" is used to identify an organization's chief staff officer. The search-and-replace function can be used to customize each document with the appropriate terms.

When customizing these documents, the user needs to consider the unique situation in which they are being used and make the necessary modifications.

Part I: Ethics and Accountability

1. Mission

Introduction

The mission statement reflects the heart of the nonprofit organization. It explains why the organization exists and what it hopes to achieve in the future. It serves as the touchstone for all decisions and activities, whether carried out by the board, staff, or volunteers. The mission statement reflects the organization's essential nature, connects to its values, shapes programs and services, and provides the foundation for all fundraising activities. It is not a policy but a statement — the written expression of the organization's purpose that is referred to as a source of guidance and motivation.

Key Elements

- A mission statement captures the reason and the need, and adds a simple, powerful statement of what the organization is doing to meet those needs.

- A clear mission statement is inspirational yet realistic, emotional as well as informative, concise and complete. It is positive in spirit and focuses on achievable accomplishments.

- Some mission statements take a practical approach and define the difference the organization makes, for whom, and how. Others create an image with just a few words. Regardless of the approach, a mission statement should be easy to remember and simple to share.

- A mission statement serves as the starting point for other overarching statements and goals, such as a tag line for marketing or a case statement for fundraising.

Practical Tips

- ✓ An organization's purpose is defined in its organizational document (e.g., articles of incorporation), often briefly and broadly, to allow for programmatic flexibility — within certain parameters — over time. Consider developing a more compelling, more articulate mission statement for regular internal and external use.

- ✓ Be sure to use the mission statement as a tool when reaching out to constituents, recruiting board members and volunteers, convincing supporters of the difference the organization is out to make, and simply explaining the primary purpose and value of the organization to any potential or present stakeholder.

Sample Mission Statements

The sample mission statements reveal different aspects of the organization through the way they are framed.

1. This simple, direct mission statement explains what the organization does and ends with a statement of a core value.

2. This straightforward mission statement defines the organization's goals and values. Although it is specific to an organization providing medical education, it is easily adapted to other types of services.

3. This mission statement identifies various services and frames them within a common goal outlined in the last item. This, too, can be adapted easily to fit different types of organizations.

SUGGESTED RESOURCES

- Angelica, Emil. *Crafting Effective Mission and Vision Statements*. St. Paul, MN: Fieldstone Alliance, 2001.

- Brinckerhoff, Peter C. *Mission-Based Management: Leading Your Not-for-Profit in the 21st Century*. New York: John Wiley & Sons, 2000.

- Grace, Kay Sprinkel. *The Nonprofit Board's Role in Setting and Advancing the Mission*. Washington, DC: BoardSource, 2003.

- Poderis, Tony. "Don't Make Your Organization's Statement Of Purpose A 'Mission Impossible.'" www.raise-funds.com/1101forum.html

2. VALUES

INTRODUCTION

Nonprofit organizations, by definition, are mission-oriented and values-driven. As boards work to gain a sense of mission and create and reaffirm mission statements, it is imperative to express the organization's values. Values are embedded in the mission and vision of the organization; they are what click with people when they read the organization's materials or experience the products and services. Like a mission statement, a values statement is not a policy, yet it serves as a guide for the organization and its staff, board, and volunteers, who deliver services to the community. It sets the standard for all aspects of the organization's programs and operations, from workplace environment and donor relations to client services and vendor relations.

KEY ELEMENTS

- An overarching theme can serve as a helpful starting point for articulating the organization's values. For example, a school for children with learning difficulties might specify a strong belief that "Having a language-based learning disability does not predict academic failure." And, a cancer support group might begin with: "People are not defined by their disease."

- A values statement should accurately reveal the organization's unique qualities and character. While values often seem universal, organizations should identify those principles and beliefs that are most important to their mission. When using common values — such as integrity, quality, trust — they should be tailored to the particular organization and the people or purpose it serves.

PRACTICAL TIPS

- ✓ The true benefit of values statements is the collective process and adoption of the values themselves. To make a values statement meaningful, the entire staff should be involved in the development phase. Active support and true ownership is always easier when those who must live by the rules have participated in their development.

- ✓ Involve the board appropriately in shaping the values statement. At the very least, the board will approve the final values statement and, of course, abide by it in its own deliberations and actions.

- ✓ In your values statement, incorporate the notion of inclusivity. Your personnel policies may already address equal employment opportunities (see Part VI: Personnel, Section 2: Equal Employment Opportunity), but non-discrimination is a much broader, values-based issue. Include your customers, clients, and members, as well as board and vendors in a wider-ranging statement about inclusivity.

SAMPLE VALUES STATEMENTS

The first three values statements are clear and concise, beginning with a generic statement and ending with one that articulates values in terms of organizational practices. The fourth sample offers a policy related to inclusivity.

1. This generic example, which describes commonly articulated values, serves as a good template for consideration and customization by other organizations.

2. This values statement distinguishes among the values that guide different aspects of the organization, from staff to services to the organization in general.

3. This sample begins with basic beliefs and then articulates how these beliefs are put into practice. It also addresses the unique role foundations play in philanthropy and the nonprofit sector.

4. This policy approaches the issue in terms of organizational inclusivity and extends to more than employment opportunities.

SUGGESTED RESOURCES

- "A Checklist for Developing a Statement of Values and Code of Ethics." www.independentsector.org/issues/ethics/code_checklist.html

- Angelica, Emil. *Crafting Effective Mission and Vision Statements*. St. Paul, MN: Fieldstone Alliance, 2001.

- Collins, Jim. "Aligning Action and Values." *Leader to Leader*. No. 1, Summer 1996. www.pfdf.org/leaderbooks/l2l/summer96/collins.html

- Grace, Kay Sprinkel. *The Nonprofit Board's Role in Setting and Advancing the Mission*. Washington, DC: BoardSource, 2003.

- Vogelsang, John D. "Values Based Organization Development." *Journal for Nonprofit Management*. Vol. 2, 1998. www.supportctr.org/values-based-organization-development.php

3. CODE OF ETHICS

INTRODUCTION

There has been increasing concern about ethical behavior in nonprofit — particularly charitable — organizations in recent years. Public scandals in the nonprofit sector have drawn attention to the need for an increased level of board accountability. In response, many organizations have developed codes of ethics. These documents encompass the values of the organization and provide a code of conduct for employees and volunteers. While a values statement, discussed above, guides the organization in a strategic, fundamental way, codes of ethics shape the actions, behaviors, and decision making of an organization in a more explicit way. Although a code of ethics by itself cannot prevent wrongdoing, it conveys a strong message both internally and externally about the culture and work of the organization.

KEY ELEMENTS

- A code of ethics serves as an overarching statement for other policies that establish standards of integrity and accountability.

- A code of ethics should outline the process and/or mechanism for implementing the defined culture and values within the organization from top to bottom.

- A code of ethics is often general in nature. Some issues, such as confidentiality, conflict of interest, and nepotism, may be addressed in separate policies (see list of contents to find samples of these more specific topics).

PRACTICAL TIPS

✓ Define what ethical behavior means for your organization, and clarify accepted professional standards.

✓ Separate staff and board issues. Board members and staff members often get confronted with different situations based on their role vis-à-vis the organization, its constituents, and the community at large.

✓ When discussing the code with staff and board members, it is often useful to provide examples of unacceptable behavior.

✓ As a way to stress the importance of the code, some organizations request a signature from board and staff members as a sign of understanding and acceptance of the standards.

✓ Once the code is established, it should be reviewed periodically by the staff and board for possible revision. In this way, the language of the code will continue to serve the expectations and needs of the organization.

SAMPLE CODES OF ETHICS

The seven samples range from very general to exceedingly specific, with each reflecting the organization's values and culture.

1. This brief statement provides broad ethical guidelines and expectations.

2. This policy establishes a formal statement about promoting ethical conduct.

3. This sample is a short statement affirming that a high level of integrity and caring is expected from the board and staff.

4. This ethics policy sets an affirmative tone through the introductory phrase of "We will do the following."

5. This code of conduct sets its standard by stating what the board and key staff will *not* do. It also includes a signature line and reporting procedures.

6. This comprehensive code of ethics covers many aspects of organizational management and oversight, beginning with a statement of integrity and including a specific section on the board.

7. This code of ethics, because it was developed in the wake of an organizational crisis that generated considerable negative publicity, takes a truly comprehensive approach to ethics. It includes the establishment of an ethics officer and committee. It is the only document in *The Nonprofit Policy Sampler* that includes the name of the contributing organization because it is best understood in the context of how, when, and why it was developed.

SUGGESTED RESOURCES

- American Bar Association Coordinating Committee. *Guide to Nonprofit Corporate Governance in the Wake of Sarbanes-Oxley.* Chicago, IL: American Bar Association, 2005.

- "Compendium of Standards, Codes, and Principles of Nonprofit and Philanthropic Organizations." www.independentsector.org/issues/ accountability/standards2.html

- Ethics Resource Center: www.ethics.org

- Kurtz, Daniel L. and Sarah E. Paul. *Managing Conflicts of Interest: A Primer for Nonprofit Boards.* Washington, DC: BoardSource, 2006.

- Ober|Kaler, attorneys at law. *The Nonprofit Legal Landscape.* Washington, DC: BoardSource, 2005.

4. CONFLICT OF INTEREST

INTRODUCTION

A conflict of interest exists when a board member or employee has a personal interest that may influence him or her when making a decision for the organization. While the law focuses primarily on financial interests and provides some guidelines, nonprofit organizations contend with a variety of potential and perceived conflicts of interest, only some of which may be detrimental to the organization. The key for nonprofit boards is *not* to try to avoid all possible conflict-of-interest situations, which would be impossible; rather, boards need to identify and follow a process for handling them effectively.

Both board members and employees must abide by conflict-of-interest policies. Generally, conflict-of-interest policies should clarify what a conflict of interest is, what board members and employees must do to disclose possible conflicts of interest, and what board members and employees should do to avoid acting inappropriately if and when a conflict of interest does arise. How an organization ensures open and honest deliberation affects all aspects of its operations and is critical to making good decisions, avoiding legal problems and public scandals, and remaining focused on the organization's mission.

KEY ELEMENTS

- Every organization needs a conflict-of-interest policy. Remember, conflicts of interest are not uncommon and not inherently illegal. Rather, they create situations that need careful attention and a process for handling them appropriately.

- Conflicts are not only financial in nature. Issue conflicts (for example, if a board member takes a position or supports another organization that is counter to the organization's mission and principles) may have to be addressed as well.

- Conflict-of-interest policies should be applicable to the board and key staff, at a minimum; they may also include other employees and key constituents with influence over the organization (e.g., major donors).

- A conflict-of-interest policy should clearly define a consistent process for dealing with conflicts. This process should include, at a minimum, disclosure and recusal. It also often includes the expectation for the board member in question to leave the room for the discussion and voting and, in extreme situations, to resign.

- Ultimately, the policy should clarify the consequences for violating the policy, which may include dismissal.

- Some organizations, instead of using the term conflict of interest, use a term *duality of interest*. A duality of interest recognizes that, under certain circumstances, even if a board member has multiple interests, those interests do not necessarily create a conflicting situation.

PRACTICAL TIPS

✓ Conflicts of interest are sometimes quite obvious and other times more obscure. To provide better guidance, consider including examples of what constitutes a conflict of interest for the organization. These examples may be lengthy, organization-specific, and/or distinguish between real, perceived, or potential conflicts.

✓ On the administrative side, determine who will maintain proper documentation of signed conflict-of-interest disclosure statements, as well as who has responsibility for determining whether or not an actual conflict of interest occurs. Often, these responsibilities are shared between the chief executive and a board committee.

✓ Busy and engaged people, like board members, are involved in various activities in the community, and these affiliations are likely to collide at times. At least annually, consider requiring board and staff members to disclose — in writing — any relationships that might constitute a conflict of interest. By openly and preemptively disclosing these potentially conflicting connections, the organization is better able to carry out proper due diligence.

SAMPLE CONFLICT-OF-INTEREST POLICIES

The extensive collection of samples provides a range of policies and forms, giving everything from general guidance on issues related to standards of operation, to detailed examples of conflicts of interest, processes for disclosure, and even foundation-specific guidelines.

1. This brief policy provides general guidelines and definitions related to conflicts of interest.

2. This solid example of a conflict-of-interest statement begins by explaining why a conflict-of-interest policy is important, and then defines key components of the policy and the process for handling conflicts.

3. This comprehensive conflict-of-interest policy follows a traditional legal format and is recommended by the IRS. Part V, section 5 of IRS Form 1023 defines who and what constitute a conflict of interest, asks questions to determine if the organization has procedures on handling conflicts, and makes recommendations on creating a conflict-of-interest policy if one does not exist.

4. This sample is a disclosure form, asking individuals to list their affiliations with other entities that might potentially affect their independent decision making.

5. This more comprehensive disclosure statement is designed to also identify potential conflicts of interest based on a more expansive definition of affiliated persons.

6. This policy acknowledges a duality of interest separate from a conflict of interest and includes a disclosure form.

7. This conflict-of-interest policy begins with a set of "whereas" clauses to provide the context for its policy, then presents the actual policy as a resolution, and concludes with an appendix with organization-specific examples of what does and does not constitute a material conflict of interest.

8. This detailed policy recognizes the potential of structural conflicts, defines the situations with clarity, outlines the entire board process, and includes an annual disclosure form.

9. This sample policy is specifically for foundation boards, which need to have a clear policy and process in place for handling conflicts that arise when board members and staff are affiliated with potential grantees. It also has two elements that may be useful for all nonprofits — guidelines for recording conflict-of-interest proceedings and issues of compensation.

10. This sample policy comes from a community foundation and includes a disclosure form for trustees to record their involvement in other community businesses and nonprofits.

SUGGESTED RESOURCES

- Brauer, Lawrence M. and Charles F. Kaiser III. "Tax-Exempt Health Care Organizations Revised Conflict of Interest Policy." www.irs.gov/pub/irs-utl/topice00.pdf

- "Conflicts of Interest at Foundations: Avoiding the Bad and Managing the Good." Washington, DC: BoardSource, 2005. www.boardsource.org/dl.asp?document_id=25

- Kurtz, Daniel L. and Sarah E. Paul. *Managing Conflicts of Interest: A Primer for Nonprofit Boards*. Washington, DC: BoardSource, 2006.

- Ober|Kaler, attorneys at law. *The Nonprofit Legal Landscape*. Washington, DC: BoardSource, 2005.

- "On the Road to a Conflict-of-Interest-Free Sector: December 2005 Question of the Month Results." www.guidestar.org/news/features/ question_dec05.jsp

5. CONFIDENTIALITY

INTRODUCTION

Nonprofit leaders may find themselves challenged to find the right balance between transparency and confidentiality. Nonprofit organizations are required by law to disclose certain information, such as their IRS Form 990 or 990-PF. In addition, many states have sunshine laws — open meeting laws — that require certain nonprofits to make at least some portions of their board meetings open to the public.

Beyond that, it becomes more complicated. On the one hand, it is often in an organization's best interest to share information with donors, stakeholders, and the general public in order to demonstrate its positive impact on the community. On the other hand, nonprofit organizations operate in a demanding and competitive environment. Like any business, they need to plan, manage, and oversee their operations internally on a regular basis. Part of the board's duty of loyalty is to maintain the confidentiality of core organizational information.

Nonprofit organizations often deal with sensitive information about clients, donors, employees, and volunteers. Confidentiality policies are important to an organization's credibility and reputation, and both board and staff should understand their responsibilities in this area.

KEY ELEMENTS

- Boards are often exposed to confidential information critical to the well-being of the organization. Information that generally is considered confidential and/or privileged includes planning documents; business and legal negotiations; client, customer, and patient records; personnel files; anonymous donor records; security guidelines; and any other matters discussed in executive sessions.

- For some nonprofits, because of their service area (e.g., domestic violence) and/or organizational complexity (e.g., hospitals), it is more efficient to proactively categorize certain documents and information as confidential. For other organizations, the board may, in briefing packets and during meetings, identify specific items that are confidential, thereby reminding board members of their commitment to confidentiality. Taken further, the board may vote on whether certain sensitive issues and/or discussions are confidential in nature.

PRACTICAL TIPS

✓ Acknowledge the contradiction between confidentiality and transparency broadly. At the same time, educate board and staff about nonprofit public disclosure requirements. Explain that confidentiality, when properly adhered to, does not contradict the organization's need to remain publicly accountable for its actions.

✓ Make the confidentiality policy part of the board member and new staff orientation.

✓ Discuss the reasons for confidentiality. By understanding the purpose, it is easier to abide by the policy.

✓ Connect the confidentiality policy to board members' duty of loyalty, which obligates them to act in the best interest of the organization.

✓ Ensure that client privilege for confidentiality is respected. Do not share any information that relates to your clients — even identification of who they are, except under certain circumstances. Confidentiality should be automatic in the case of lawyer-client or accountant-client relationships.

✓ In the confidentiality policy, recognize legal requirements for confidential records (e.g., HIPAA, personnel files, national security).

SAMPLE CONFIDENTIALITY POLICIES

The six confidentiality policies range from overarching guidelines to detailed documents, and they take into account some concerns specific to certain kinds of nonprofits.

1. This very brief policy is a basic statement of values relating to confidentiality.

2. This general policy provides board and staff members with broad guidelines for handling confidential information.

3. This policy identifies particular information that is confidential, and includes a disciplinary policy for staff. While parts of it are specific to membership organizations, the scope and intent of it is relevant for all organizations.

4. This policy provides more specificity about what information must be kept confidential. While parts of it are specific to foundations and their grantees, the scope and intent of it is relevant for all organizations.

5. This specific policy outlines what information (e.g., names and addresses) and documents may not be disclosed. A few items are specific to community foundations, but the level of detail could be easily adapted for other nonprofits.

6. This confidentiality policy explicitly states what information employees are prohibited from disclosing during and after their employment, and it requires a signature.

SUGGESTED RESOURCES

- Frey, Jeannie C. and George W. Overton, eds. *Guidebook for Directors of Nonprofit Corporations.* Chicago, IL: American Bar Association, 2002.

- Kurtz, Daniel L. and Sarah E. Paul. *Managing Conflicts of Interest: A Primer for Nonprofit Boards.* Washington, DC: BoardSource, 2006.

6. WHISTLEBLOWER PROTECTION

INTRODUCTION

The Sarbanes-Oxley Act of 2002 makes it a federal crime for any organization — nonprofit and for-profit — to retaliate against a "whistleblower" who reports illegal or unacceptable activity. It also requires publicly traded companies to establish a confidential process for reporting misuse of the organization's financial assets.

In practice, it is difficult to separate the prohibition against retaliation from the reporting process. So, most whistleblower policies address both. They are also being used to address other improprieties, such as discrimination and sexual harassment. Individuals who witness any kind of unsuitable behavior must feel free to speak out. Nonprofit leaders — board and senior management together — should take complaints seriously, undertake an investigation, and rectify the situation.

KEY ELEMENTS

- The whistleblower policy should state, unequivocally, that fraudulent actions are not tolerated. It may also apply to other improprieties.

- A confidential reporting mechanism sends a message to the entire staff that fraud is not tolerated and that whistleblowers are protected. That mechanism might be automated, such as online services or phone lines. Or, it may include a hierarchy of levels within the organization, from the human resource manager and the chief executive to the audit committee and the board chair.

PRACTICAL TIPS

- ✓ To ensure clarity, provide definitions in the whistleblower policy that range from identifying what allegations are governed by the policy to what constitutes retaliation.

- ✓ The policy should also outline a clear and consistent practice for reporting alleged violations. This process should be explicit about how and to whom complaints are submitted.

- ✓ A whistleblower policy functions as an extension of a code of ethics and a parallel process to complaint procedures (see Part VI: Personnel, Section 6: Complaints). In developing the policy and the process, consider its relationship to these other policies.

SAMPLE WHISTLEBLOWER PROTECTION POLICIES

The four samples provide different approaches to reporting procedures, whistleblower protection, and defining fraudulent activity versus misbehavior.

1. This policy is written in simple language and focuses on the intent behind whistleblower protection.

2. This sample provides clear definitions and provisions for handling allegations of misconduct while protecting the organization under difficult circumstances.

3. This sample expands the list of improprieties that are subject to the whistleblower policy to include fraudulent actions *and* actions that violate other codes of conduct.

4. This policy provides a description of reporting procedures in further detail.

SUGGESTED RESOURCES

- American Bar Association Coordinating Committee. *Guide to Nonprofit Corporate Governance in the Wake of Sarbanes-Oxley.* Chicago, IL: American Bar Association, 2005.

- Ober|Kaler, attorneys at law. *The Nonprofit Legal Landscape.* Washington, DC: BoardSource, 2005.

- Office of Compliance Assistance Policy. *Employment Law Guide.* Washington DC: U.S. Department of Labor, 2005.

- "The Sarbanes-Oxley Act and Its Implications for Nonprofit Organizations." Washington, DC: BoardSource and Independent Sector, revised in 2006.

7. RECORD RETENTION AND DOCUMENT DESTRUCTION

INTRODUCTION

Record retention and document destruction are distinct but complementary issues. Record retention balances the need for an organization to maintain accurate and appropriate files with the challenge of limited physical and electronic space for archives. All businesses need to keep documents that preserve institutional history for strategic planning, regulatory compliance, and legal purposes.

The Sarbanes-Oxley Act of 2002 forbids purging of documents when any organization — nonprofit or for-profit — is under federal investigation. Document destruction policies provide guidelines for the proper disposal of records and prevent destruction of relevant documentation if the organization is involved in litigation.

It is a federal crime to alter, cover up, falsify, or destroy any document to prevent its use in an official proceeding. Retention and destruction policies are helpful under any circumstances. When already in place, these policies not only help nonprofits retain appropriate historical and legal documentation, but they also clarify the steps to take if a federal investigation ever takes place.

KEY ELEMENTS

- The document retention policy should cover employee records, accounting and tax records (e.g., bank statements, audits, IRS forms), legal documents (e.g., articles of incorporation, tax-exempt application, the determination letter, contracts, intellectual property documents, real estate records), board-related records (minutes, policies, resolutions), and e-mails and voicemails.

- In some cases, the applicable retention period is dictated by statute. In other cases, it is a matter of judgment. (Accordingly, in a few cases, the recommended retention periods for the sample policies may differ slightly.)

- When under federal investigation or where litigation is either ongoing or imminent — or even if that becomes a possibility — state clearly that all document destruction must stop and documents must be preserved.

PRACTICAL TIPS

✓ State that the purpose of the policy is to help establish organizational procedures for the retention, maintenance, and destruction of records, consistent with applicable legal requirements.

✓ Indicate the legal and/or desired retention periods for all records (and double-check with legal counsel regarding retention periods for your organization).

✓ Retention of various business documents is mandated by law. Become familiar with these requirements, as the retention period varies depending on the document.

✓ Equal care should be given to electronic documents and voicemail. Network and individual computer backup systems need systematic attention and should be part of regular risk management.

✓ Maintain a good filing system: Categorize various records appropriately so they are easy to find.

SAMPLE RECORD RETENTION AND DOCUMENT DESTRUCTION POLICIES

The four samples address both record retention and document destruction guidelines, with two policies focusing on retention specifically, one on destruction, and one on both issues.

1. This brief document retention policy is framed as part of compliance with Sarbanes-Oxley; it includes a list of documents and time periods.

2. This straightforward policy — relevant to for-profit companies but helpful because of its additional details — provides more specific guidance for different kinds of documents, and it requires an employee's signature.

3. This straightforward policy covers both document retention and destruction.

4. This short policy provides explicit guidelines on how to destroy documents containing confidential information, which is particularly important for certain kinds of health and social service providers that are subject to government regulation regarding client privacy.

SUGGESTED RESOURCES

• American Bar Association Coordinating Committee. *Guide to Nonprofit Corporate Governance in the Wake of Sarbanes-Oxley*. Chicago, IL: American Bar Association, 2005.

• "Document Retention & Destruction Policies: What You Don't Know *Can* Hurt You." www.lexisnexis.com/applieddiscovery/lawlibrary/whitePapers/ ADI_WP_DocRetentionDestruction.pdf

- Ober|Kaler, attorneys at law. *The Nonprofit Legal Landscape*. Washington, DC: BoardSource, 2005.

- "The Sarbanes-Oxley Act and Its Implications for Nonprofit Organizations." Washington, DC: BoardSource and Independent Sector, revised in 2006.

Part II: Board and Board Members

1. ROLE OF THE BOARD

INTRODUCTION

A nonprofit board is well-served to establish policies to guide it. Policies relating to the overall role of the board remind board members that they are part of a group with authority over, and liability for, the organization. These policies often involve duties of the board as a whole and/or of individual board members. While these documents take many forms — from general lists, to job descriptions, to letters of understanding — they serve a common function: to clearly communicate the board's responsibilities as a governing body (also see Part II: Board and Board Members, Section 2: Board Member Agreements).

KEY ELEMENTS

- Defining accountability for the organization is a key element in defining the board's role.

- While there are many ways to describe the role of the board, its fundamental responsibilities derive from three duties — care, loyalty, and obedience. These duties mean that board members must make prudent, educated, and independent decisions; place the organization above their personal preferences; and remain faithful to the mission of the organization.

- The policy should speak to the board as a group with collective duties. Board responsibilities fall into three broad areas: setting direction, overseeing the affairs of the organization, and ensuring adequate resources.

PRACTICAL TIPS

✓ Draft these policies to include legal requirements, but frame and style them according to your own board culture.

✓ Realize that policies evolve as the organization and the board evolve. Start with the basics but ensure that these documents are constantly reviewed and amended, and new policies are added as they become relevant.

SAMPLE ROLE OF THE BOARD STATEMENTS

The sample policies provided range in style, offering different approaches. Some focus on the team only, some include specific responsibilities of individual board members, some stress accountability, and others spell out general expectations.

1. This short statement defines the role of the board and sets clear expectations for board members.

2. This board code of conduct provides standards for what is expected of individual board members.

3. This statement is a well-organized list of responsibilities for the full board.

4. This statement elaborates on general and individual board responsibilities by outlining the areas of board focus and stating detailed expectations for fundraising and committee service.

5. This list of board responsibilities defines the board's role in key activities, sets expectations of individual board member participation, and outlines basic board operations (e.g., number of meetings, conflicts of interest, etc.).

SUGGESTED RESOURCES

- Chait, Richard P., William P. Ryan, and Barbara E. Taylor. *Governance as Leadership: Reframing the Work of Nonprofit Boards*. New York and Washington, DC: John Wiley & Sons and BoardSource, 2005.

- Eadie, Douglas C. *Extraordinary Board Leadership: The Seven Keys to High-Impact Governance*. Gaithersburg, MD: Aspen Publishers, 2001.

- Hopkins, Bruce R. *Legal Responsibilities of Nonprofit Boards*. Washington, DC: BoardSource, 2003.

- Ingram, Richard T. *Ten Basic Responsibilities of Nonprofit Boards*. Washington, DC: BoardSource, 2003.

- Robinson, Maureen K. *Nonprofit Boards That Work*. New York: John Wiley & Sons, 2001.

- *The Source: Twelve Principles of Governance That Power Exceptional Boards*. Washington, DC: BoardSource, 2005.

2. BOARD MEMBER AGREEMENTS

INTRODUCTION

A board member agreement is the promise a board member makes when accepting a position for nonprofit board service. It is not a legal document but an internal agreement, asserting the board member's commitment to the organization in addition to an understanding of the general board responsibilities (as discussed in Part II: Board and Board Members, Section 1: Role of the Board). These documents are useful tools for recruitment purposes in that they clearly state what board service is all about; sometimes, they supplement more holistic board job descriptions.

KEY ELEMENTS

- A board member agreement may list specific expectations for board service. Commonly found items include fundraising and personal giving, activity in committees, attendance in meetings, and promises to keep confidential issues confidential.

- If the organization has a separate job description for the board and/or board members, this agreement often focuses on individual pledges to serve as an active and committed member of the board.

- It should be clear that regardless of whether board members sign any type of "contract" with a nonprofit organization, state nonprofit corporation laws in all states automatically impose certain fiduciary duties on nonprofit board members. Board members should be made aware of those legal duties and obligations when they assume their positions. (The typical fiduciary duties imposed by law include the duty of care and the duty of loyalty, as discussed in Part II: Board and Board Members, Section 1: Role of the Board, both of which require a certain level of diligence and prohibit conflicts of interest.)

PRACTICAL TIPS

- ✓ The tone of the document should reflect the organization's values and the board's culture. What this document is called — contract, agreement, statement of understanding — will shape its style and presentation.

- ✓ Individual board members are often asked to sign the document to stress the importance of their commitment. They may do this once, when they join the board, or it may be an annual reaffirmation.

- ✓ To avoid the sense of one-sided expectations, it is useful to include in the agreement what the organization provides for the members of the board: protection from liability through D&O insurance coverage, accurate and timely reports to facilitate decision making, and gratitude and appreciation for the volunteer service.

SAMPLE BOARD MEMBER AGREEMENTS

The samples provide options for stressing the importance of board member expectations, in addition to the basic roles and responsibilities of the board. As suggested above, some also include the organization's commitment back to the board member.

1. This brief board member job description translates general board duties into individual board member expectations.

2. This short contract begins with the organization's commitment to the board and then outlines expectations of board service.

3. This brief statement of understanding uses a series of "I will" statements.

4. This lengthier sample covers general responsibilities, but also establishes minimum financial contributions and an expectation to resign if a board member is no longer able to adhere to this contract.

5. This document stresses the moral, fiscal, and legal role of board members. Besides listing expectations of individuals, it also states what the organization will provide in return.

- "A Board Member Contract." *Board Café.* 2003.
  www.compasspoint.org/boardcafe/details.php?id=30

- Hughes, Sandra R., Berit M. Lakey, and Marla J. Bobowick. *The Board Building Cycle: Nine Steps to Finding, Recruiting, and Engaging Nonprofit Board Members.* Washington, DC: BoardSource, 2000.

- Ingram, Richard T. *Ten Basic Responsibilities of Nonprofit Boards.* Washington, DC: BoardSource, 2003.

- Lakey, Berit M., Sandra R. Hughes, and Outi Flynn. *Governance Committee.* Washington, DC: BoardSource, 2004.

3. BOARD CHAIR JOB DESCRIPTIONS

INTRODUCTION

The job of the board chair is one of the most challenging roles in the nonprofit world. A successful chair inspires a shared vision for the organization and its work, builds and nurtures future board leadership, and manages the work of the board. This position demands exceptional commitment to the organization, first-rate leadership qualities, and personal integrity. For many boards, success may rest heavily on the individual chosen to lead it.

KEY ELEMENTS

- As the chief volunteer officer, the board chair's duties run from managing the board to working closely with the chief executive. Additional duties may relate to his or her role as a spokesperson for the organization. If the board has an executive committee (see Part VIII: Committees, Section 4: Executive Committee), the board chair also chairs this committee.

- In functioning as the team leader of the board, the board chair sets goals for the board, involves all board members in the work of the board (during meetings and through committee assignments), serves as the contact for all board members on board issues, and facilitates board meetings.

- In working closely with the chief executive, the board chair may be assigned responsibility for managing the overall board-chief executive relationship, such as developing meeting agendas and coordinating the executive's annual performance review.

PRACTICAL TIPS

- ✓ The chair's role is usually defined in the bylaws, but a separate job description should be created to outline the duties in more detail.

- ✓ The official title of the chief volunteer officer varies from organization to organization. The terms "chair" and "president" are the same, and the organization's bylaws should dictate which is used. The most common — and least confusing — title is that of "chair." This prevents confusion with the chief staff officer, who may have a title of president and chief executive officer.

✓ If the expectations for the board chair become too demanding and the position too time-consuming, it will be difficult to recruit new chairs. Often, some of the responsibilities and tasks can be shared with other board officers to make the position more reasonable for a volunteer.

SAMPLE BOARD CHAIR JOB DESCRIPTIONS

The seven job descriptions run from brief and broad to formal and focused.

1. This bylaws clause broadly defines the role of the board chair.

2. This short statement lists the main duties of the chair as they relate to the functions of the board.

3. This brief sample clarifies the authority of the chair as the leader of the board and the manager of board practices.

4. This basic list outlines expectations for the chair of an organization that does not have a large staff.

5. This brief job description elaborates on core board chair duties towards the organization, chief executive, board process, and community.

6. This more comprehensive job description outlines the various functions of the board chair position in relation to overall board responsibility categories.

7. This detailed job description addresses all aspects of the board chair's position, from purpose to qualifications.

SUGGESTED RESOURCES

- Dietel, William M. and Linda R. Dietel. *The Board Chair Handbook*. Washington, DC: BoardSource, 2001.

- Gale, Robert L. *Leadership Roles in Nonprofit Governance*. Washington, DC: BoardSource, 2003.

- Ingram, Richard T. *Ten Basic Responsibilities of Nonprofit Boards*. Washington, DC: BoardSource, 2003.

- Light, Mark. *The Strategic Board: The Step-by-Step Guide to High-Impact Governance*. New York: John Wiley & Sons, 2001.

- *The Source: Twelve Principles of Governance That Power Exceptional Boards*. Washington, DC: BoardSource, 2005.

4. OTHER BOARD OFFICER JOB DESCRIPTIONS

INTRODUCTION

The most common board officers, beyond the chair, are vice chair, secretary, and treasurer. These positions are most frequently defined by state laws. The law may also indicate whether one individual can hold more than one officer position. In addition, some organizations have a chair-elect, which is one way to secure future leadership for the organization.

Specific officer duties may vary greatly from board to board. Particularly as the organization hires new and different staff, it is important to review and update officer job descriptions to reflect any changes in their focus.

KEY ELEMENTS

- Vice Chair: The office of vice chair provides the board with additional and substitute leadership. The vice chair generally fills in for the chair when the chair is absent and/or must leave the position permanently and without warning. The vice chair often takes on special projects, and some boards may divide various duties among two or more vice chairs.

- Chair-Elect: In some cases, a board may determine a candidate to succeed the board chair before the chair's term in office has concluded. The chair-elect may be given specific tasks, such as heading up the strategic planning task force. This position may provide a useful leadership development training ground and help to ensure a smoother transition when he or she assumes the role of board chair. In many professional associations, the chair-elect may be elected or appointed by the membership at large.

- Treasurer: The key volunteer financial management role in nonprofit organizations is the treasurer. The treasurer is responsible for overseeing financial operations to make certain that things are done in an appropriate fashion. In staffed organizations, the financial records are kept by the chief financial officer, controller, or accountant. In smaller organizations the treasurer may have hands-on responsibilities.

- Secretary: Depending upon the organization's size and staff, the job of recording minutes can fall to either a board member or a staff member. In the event that a staff member fills the position, the board's official secretary should review the minutes prior to distribution. In addition, the board secretary acts as the custodian of the board's records, although in most circumstances the board's important documents are kept in the organization's offices.

PRACTICAL TIPS

- ✓ As in the case for the chair, the primary roles for these officer positions are generally defined in the bylaws; however, consider creating separate job descriptions to describe the specific responsibilities of the officers.

✓ On some boards, the individual serving as vice chair may naturally assume the role of chair. In order for this assumption to be automatic, it must be defined that way in the board's policies.

✓ It is possible, and increasingly common, to combine the secretary and treasurer into one officer position. However, separate individuals should hold the chair and treasurer positions.

✓ Particularly for reasons of accountability and balance, and increasingly to meet the requirements of the nonprofit corporation laws of some states, consider appointing an audit committee to act as the main liaison to the outside auditor, electing someone other than the treasurer to serve as chair of the finance committee (see also Part VIII: Committees, Section 2: Financial Committees).

SAMPLE JOB DESCRIPTIONS FOR OTHER BOARD OFFICERS

The sample job descriptions include variations on common themes, with the first in each category capturing the basic responsibilities of that position.

1. This very brief job description defines the purpose of the vice chair simply as presiding over the board in the chair's absence.

2. This short job description defines the role of the vice chair as supporting the chair.

3. This sample delegates specific responsibilities to the chair-elect, including acting as liaison to the organization's chapters, if applicable.

4. This brief job description outlines responsibilities commonly assigned to the treasurer and includes chair duties for the finance committee.

5. This sample provides a detailed list of tasks for the treasurer, including working with the organization's regional chapters, if any.

6. This document is a full-fledged job description for a board treasurer, complete with qualifications and a recommendation for providing opportunities for leadership development.

7. This job description outlines fiscal duties assigned to the treasurer in an all-volunteer organization.

8. This short sample assigns the treasurer role to the chief staff financial officer. This position is a nonvoting board position.

9. This job description focuses on the secretary's responsibility for documenting board meetings.

10. This job description frames the duties of the secretary as the custodian of organizational documents.

11. This sample delegates certain secretarial responsibilities to a staff member who serves as a nonvoting member of the board.

Suggested Resources

- "Board Essentials." BoardSource. www.boardsource.org/Knowledge.asp?ID=3.1014

- "Board Officers Sample Job Descriptions." Minnesota Council of Nonprofits. www.mncn.org/info/template_gov.htm#bd%20officer%20sample%20job%20description

- Light, Mark. *The Strategic Board: The Step-by-Step Guide to High-Impact Governance.* New York: John Wiley & Sons, 2001.

5. Compensation of Board Members

Introduction

Unlike their counterparts who serve on boards of for-profit corporations, nonprofit board members are volunteers who are not usually compensated for their time. However, many boards have policies authorizing reimbursement of certain expenses. And, in some organizations, the full board or senior board officers may in fact receive compensation for their services.

Key Elements

- A compensation policy either states clearly that compensation is *not* provided or outlines acceptable fees for board service. Separate policies address reimbursement for expenses (see Part II: Board and Board Members, Section 6: Board Member Expense Reimbursement) and how to handle potential payment for additional professional services.

- According to the *BoardSource 2004 Governance Index*, only 2 percent of board members are compensated for their board service. But, even if board members are not compensated, a statement to that effect is helpful. This can avoid future misunderstandings and could be used during the recruitment process to manage expectations.

- If any board members are compensated, the policy should state that this compensation is approved by the board.

Practical Tips

- ✓ Compensating board members may result in a loss of protection from personal liability available only to volunteer directors. Check state law before proceeding.

- ✓ Compensation is not illegal, but if the board decides to compensate its members, the pay must be reasonable and due diligence must be followed. Do the research to find out what other, similar organizations pay their board members.

✓ Payment for non-governance services and financial transactions for business purposes between a board member and the organization is treated differently than compensation for board service. Board members may be paid for performing a professional service for the organization that is outside of general board responsibilities. For these situations, establish a separate policy to address these kinds of potential conflict-of-interest situations and provide guidance on how they can be handled (e.g., sending out RFPs for bids). For more information, see Part I: Ethics and Accountability, Section 4: Conflict of Interest.

✓ Remind board members that fees for service (not reimbursement for expenses) are taxable income and should be reported by each individual in his or her own tax returns.

SAMPLE BOARD COMPENSATION POLICIES

Policies related to board member compensation tend to be brief, and they are always very explicit. The first three policies are for those boards that do not compensate members for board service; the last two are for those that do.

1. This is a short, straightforward statement of no compensation.

2. This statement, excerpted from the bylaws, allows payment to directors who perform professional services, such as accounting or legal services.

3. This sample statement defines procedures for handling both hiring and compensating board members for their professional services.

4. This statement provides for board member compensation based on attendance at meetings and events related to board service.

5. This sample defines compensation solely based on meeting attendance.

SUGGESTED RESOURCES

- Ahn, Christine, Pablo Eisenberg, and Channapha Khamvongsa. *Foundation Trustee Fees: Uses and Abuses*. Washington, DC: The Center for Public and Nonprofit Leadership, Georgetown Public Policy Institute, September 2003.

- Cohen, Rick. "Time to Stop Excusing the Inexcusable: Foundation Trustees Who Play By Their Own Rules." *The Nonprofit Quarterly*. Winter 2003.

- "Contemplating Trustee Compensation." *Association of Small Foundations Newsletter*. Spring 2005.

- Kieffer, Mike. "Trustee Compensation: In Your Board's Future?" *Chicago Hospital News*. September 2005.

- Orlikoff, James E. and Kevin K. Murphy. "Face Off: Board Member Compensation." *Board Member*. March 2004.

- Panel on the Nonprofit Sector. *Strengthening Transparency, Governance, Account-ability of Charitable Organizations. A Supplement to the Final Report to Congress and the Nonprofit Sector.* Independent Sector, 2006.

6. BOARD MEMBER EXPENSE REIMBURSEMENT

INTRODUCTION

Along with compensation policies, expense reimbursement policies are important because they specify who can be reimbursed for what expenses. Particularly, when required to travel to meetings or annual conferences, board members need guidelines for acceptable expenses. Different organizations take different approaches to reimbursing board members. Some expect board members to cover their own expenses; others will provide reimbursement upon request, but only up to a specified amount; still others provide per diems to all board members.

KEY ELEMENTS

- When a board member pays for supplies and materials for additional work as a volunteer for the organization (i.e., apart from the traditional role of board member), the nonprofit often reimburses him or her for actual expenses approved, incurred, requested, and documented.

- In general, it is impermissible — and sometimes unethical — to pay for a board member's spouse's travel to meetings and events because the attendance of the spouse at a nonprofit function is not considered necessary (unless the spouse is representing the organization on official business and has bona fide duties to perform). Otherwise, this becomes an issue of compensation (see Part II: Board and Board Members, Section 5: Compensation of Board Members).

PRACTICAL TIPS

- ✓ In the reimbursement policy, clarify the acceptable parameters for reimbursement, such as class of airfare, level of accommodations, gas mileage rates, etc.

- ✓ Consider the fact that some nonprofits rely on government reimbursement policies.

SAMPLE BOARD MEMBER EXPENSE REIMBURSEMENT POLICIES

The various policies are arranged in order of general to specific and short to long.

1. This brief policy is a clear, generic policy that lets the board member decide whether he or she requests reimbursement.

2. This brief policy recognizes that travel expenses may be an exceptional burden for some board members and provides a discreet method for requesting reimbursement.

3. This basic policy addresses government regulations and provides some parameters for reimbursement, such as per diems and official events.

4. This more detailed sample policy defines what constitutes acceptable expenses for reimbursement.

5. This comprehensive policy provides considerable details about who and what may be covered, and procedures for getting reimbursed.

SUGGESTED RESOURCE

- Panel on the Nonprofit Sector. *Strengthening Transparency, Governance, Accountability of Charitable Organizations. A Supplement to the Final Report to Congress and the Nonprofit Sector.* Independent Sector, 2006.

7. BOARD SELF-ASSESSMENT

INTRODUCTION

The objective of board self-assessment is to help the board improve its own work. It allows board members to better understand their own roles and responsibilities and how they can more effectively fulfill their obligations. The self-assessment process can develop the board's team-building skills, provide structure for problem solving, and increase accountability within the organization.

Simply going through the process is not enough. The board needs to analyze and learn from the results, and incorporate improvements in its future behavior and structure. The board's policies on self-assessment may clarify whether and/or how individual board member performance evaluation is incorporated. Equally, the board may have policies on meeting and committee evaluations.

KEY ELEMENTS

- Self-assessment does not need to be an annual event, but the policy should state the objectives of regular performance evaluation and desired frequency.

- The policy needs to clarify that the assessment is necessary for reappointment before terms are renewed. This applies to board members and officers.

- The assessment may be carried out by the governance committee; the policy may provide an option to hire an outside facilitator to help with the discussions and aid in the administration of the self-assessment process.

Practical Tips

✓ Get each board member's buy-in in order to make board self-assessment a true group effort. Without consensus, the board simply won't participate. Members should be assured that their answers to the questionnaire will remain confidential and that the objective of the exercise is not to be punitive but to improve the board's future performance.

✓ If this is the board's first self-assessment effort, a task force should be formed to explore how others have done it and what tools they have used. In addition, the board should determine how individual board member evaluation is included for the purpose of self-reflection.

✓ Adequate time should be devoted to planning for a board self-assessment — starting well ahead of time in order to ensure that board members may have the proper time set aside to complete the assessment. A date should also be agreed upon for a board retreat to discuss the results.

✓ The board should ensure that the final recommendations that come from the board retreat discussions will be implemented by creating proper follow-up procedures. Board members should be provided with possibilities for self-improvement and clarified duties and expectations.

Sample Board Self-Assessment Policies

The brief sample statements do not set forth the process and expansive procedures for board self-assessment, but concentrate on the simple importance of this practice.

1. This very simple statement commits the board to a regular self-assessment.

2. This brief policy provides guidelines on what and who will be evaluated, including individual board members.

3. This policy ties board self-assessment to the assessment of the organization.

4. This sample sets the process for an annual self-assessment of the board as a group. It is not an assessment of the individual members.

Suggested Resources

- Holland, Thomas P. and Myra Blackmon. *Measuring Board Effectiveness: A Tool for Strengthening Your Board.* Washington, DC: BoardSource, 2000.

- Lakey, Berit M. and George Hofheimer. *Credit Union Board Self-Assessment: A Research Study.* Madison, WI, and Washington, DC: CUES and BoardSource, 2004.

- Millesen, Judith L. and Berit M. Lakey. "The Nonprofit Board Self-Assessment Process: Lessons from the Field." Washington, DC: BoardSource, 1999.

- *Self-Assessment of the Board.* Online Tool. Washington, DC: BoardSource, 2004.

Part III: Chief Executive

1. CHIEF EXECUTIVE JOB DESCRIPTIONS

INTRODUCTION

While the board is ultimately responsible for the organization's mission and strategy, the chief executive is the executor — and often the main architect — of that strategy. The chief executive is responsible for the day-to-day leadership of the organization and for its effective management.

Many people feel that the most important duty of a nonprofit board is to hire the right chief executive and supervise him or her well. Before hiring a chief executive, the board needs to clarify the responsibilities of the position and the qualifications of the person who will fill it. Chief executive job descriptions vary a great deal depending on the type of organization, field of service, staff size, and other factors.

While the chief executive is responsible for running the organization's daily affairs, he or she also has a major leadership role in helping the board do its job in the best possible manner. Board development is important and it often falls on the chief executive's shoulders, as he or she has the easiest access to necessary information and governance-related resources. Working closely with the governance committee and the board chair, the chief executive can help the board fulfill its potential.

KEY ELEMENTS

- Implicitly, if not explicitly, the board delegates daily management to the chief executive through the job description. The job description outlines the leadership framework for the chief executive to manage the daily operations of the organization. It defines the board's expectations and guidelines within which the chief executive must accomplish his or her duties.

- The chief executive's job description usually defines overall responsibility for functional areas within the organization, such as strategic direction, financial performance, personnel, and communications.

- Job descriptions should clarify the lines of authority so that the board and chief executive are clear on the chain of command. More specifically, they often articulate the role of the chief executive as the board's sole employee.

PRACTICAL TIPS

- ✓ While this publication uses the term "chief executive," other organizations may choose to refer to the chief staff officer as the executive director, president, chief executive officer, or director.

- ✓ A clear job description lays the groundwork for annual goals and performance reviews. Review and update the job description regularly as part of the chief executive's performance evaluation. As the organization evolves, the chief executive's responsibilities may also need to be adjusted. Always have a current job description available in the event of an unexpected change in leadership.

✓ As long as the state law does not invalidate the intention, a written employment contract (or memorandum of agreement) provides security to the chief executive, the board, and the organization. Clarify the job description and compensation terms in writing to ensure that mutual expectations are clear from the outset of the relationship.

✓ The job description should mention the chief executive's role as the governance partner with the board and provide specifics about this responsibility. To stress the importance of board development, indicate clearly how the chief executive is involved in recruitment of board members, orientation, continuous education, and shaping productive board meetings.

SAMPLE CHIEF EXECUTIVE JOB DESCRIPTIONS

The six job descriptions, presented from shortest to longest, cover the chief executive's duties in relationship with the board, staff, and overall organizational success.

1. This short, general job description emphasizes the chief executive's authority in managing staff and operations.

2. This concise job description delegates overall responsibility to the chief executive and calls attention to expectations of the board.

3. This simple job description articulates the basic responsibilities of the chief executive, both as the manager of the organization and a partner to the board.

4. This sample assigns responsibilities to the chief executive in specific functional areas.

5. This job description frames the chief executive's authority and responsibilities in relationship to the board, operations, staff, and the community.

6. This more specific sample defines expectations related not only to performance but also to experience and credentials.

SUGGESTED RESOURCES

- Albert, Sheila. *Hiring the Chief Executive: A Practical Guide to the Search and Selection Process.* Washington, DC: BoardSource, 2000.

- Carlson, Mim and Margaret Donohoe. *The Executive Director's Survival Guide: Thriving as a Nonprofit Leader.* San Francisco: Jossey-Bass, 2003.

- Eadie, Douglas C. *The Board-Savvy CEO: How to Build a Strong, Positive Relationship with Your Board.* Washington, DC: BoardSource, 2001.

- Linnell, Deborah, Zora Radosevich, and Jonathan Spack. *Executive Director's Guide: The Guide for Successful Nonprofit Management.* Boston, MA: United Way of Massachusetts Bay, 2002.

- Moyers, Richard L. *The Nonprofit Chief Executive's Ten Basic Responsibilities.* Washington, DC: BoardSource, 2006.

- *The Source: Twelve Principles of Governance That Power Exceptional Boards.* Washington, DC: BoardSource, 2005.

2. CHIEF EXECUTIVE PERFORMANCE EVALUATION

INTRODUCTION

Although the board delegates management and administrative duties to the chief executive, this does not excuse the board from overall responsibility for overseeing the organization. This oversight includes ensuring that the right person is running the organization at the right time and in the right way. An annual performance review is one of the most effective ways for the board to carry out this duty.

A properly administered chief executive performance evaluation can benefit the chief executive, the board, and the entire organization. Out of this important process, the chief executive gains constructive feedback on his or her performance and the board has the opportunity to measure the organization's progress towards its objectives and previously set annual goals.

The evaluation process helps to enhance the communication between the board and the chief executive. It facilitates the board's oversight function while providing the board with a concrete opportunity to support the chief executive.

KEY ELEMENTS

- An effective performance evaluation begins with a mutually understood process. The board needs to determine the appropriate role for the board chair, individual board members, and any committee. It should also address how the chief executive will participate in the process and what kind of evaluation tool to use.

- The performance evaluation should take into account the chief executive's job description, annual goals and objectives, and any other relevant factors identified or approved by the board. The executive's annual goals and objectives should be closely tied to the organization's annual goals and objectives.

- The evaluation should include the chief executive's own self-assessment as well as the board's evaluation of his or her performance. The full board needs to review both.

- The evaluation should be conducted annually and documented in writing, particularly where the outcome is adverse and/or could lead to dismissal. In all cases, the assessment will provide a permanent record that can be referred to by both the chief executive and the board, greatly increasing clarity and certainty.

- The assessment process should be separated from compensation (see also Part III: Chief Executive, Section 3: Executive Compensation) even if performance is a key element in setting or reviewing the compensation level of the chief executive. Compensation should not drive evaluation; it should be discussed independently after coming to a mutual agreement on evaluation results.

✓ Consider conducting the evaluation towards (or shortly after) the end of the fiscal year in order to tie annual goals to organizational performance.

✓ The board should provide the chief executive with frequent and constructive feedback. Even if a formal review process takes place annually, both the board and the chief executive should communicate throughout the year to highlight early warning signs and interim accomplishments.

✓ In theory, the chief executive's annual goals should be developed in collaboration with the board. In some cases it may be more efficient for the chief executive to present the board with proposed goals for consideration.

SAMPLE CHIEF EXECUTIVE PERFORMANCE EVALUATION POLICIES

The sample policies discuss various aspects of the process, from how to set expectations to who should be involved.

1. This brief statement outlines specific steps in the annual review process, as well as the role of officers, the full board, and the chief executive in the process.

2. This policy stresses the purpose of the performance review and delegates the process to the executive committee.

3. This policy statement defines the chief executive's goals as the organization's goals and provides general guidelines for the performance review.

SUGGESTED RESOURCES

• *CEO Evaluation: Navigating a New Relationship With the Board.* Mercer Delta Consulting, 2003.

• Dubois, Philip L. "Regular Performance Reviews Show Someone Is 'Minding the Store.'" *Trustee.* May/June 2004.

• Mintz, Joshua. "It's Lonely at the Top: Why Board Assessment of the Chief Executive is Critical to the Executive's — And the Organization's — Success." www.boardsource.org

• Mintz, Joshua and Jane Pierson. *Assessment of the Chief Executive, Revised.* Washington, DC: BoardSource, 2005.

3. EXECUTIVE COMPENSATION

INTRODUCTION

The chief executive's compensation package is an important component of a board's responsibility for managing the executive. Putting together a compensation package is a complex activity. It is tied to who the chief executive is expected to be as a professional and to what the chief executive is expected to do for the organization. While very personal for those involved, it is also very public; if over $50,000, the total amount of compensation must be disclosed on the IRS Form 990 and it must comply with stringent legal requirements.

KEY ELEMENTS

- Compensation includes salary and benefits. When developing a compensation policy, the board should list all components of the package. Often, the original employment contract (if any) establishes the chief executive's base compensation, and the board determines annual raises and bonuses each year. All compensation and benefits should be shown in the employment contract; there should be no unlisted, "off-agreement" benefits.

- Compensation is linked to experience, performance, and industry. A compensation policy might list those factors that the board feels are most important, such as prior experience and education level. It should also establish performance goals and compensation adjustments based on accomplishments. Lastly, it should take into account the complexity of the organization, requirements of the job, and market rates.

- A compensation policy should also address the process for determining the chief executive's compensation, such as who communicates with the chief executive, how adjustments will be determined (e.g., cost of living, merit increases, bonus rewards), researching compensation in comparable organizations, and use of external consultants.

- Fair and reasonable compensation is one of the key elements to attract and retain the most qualified chief executive for the organization. While the full board is responsible for determining appropriate compensation, it may delegate certain tasks — such as negotiating with the chief executive (during the hiring process) and reviewing comparable salaries — to a committee or an independent consultant (see also Part VIII: Committees, Section 5: Other Common Committees). The full board or a committee of the board must approve the final compensation package.

- The policy should be developed to satisfy the IRS Intermediate Sanctions safe harbor requirements of independent decision making, reliance on comparables, and documentation. (See Internal Revenue Code section 4958 and the regulations thereunder.) The Intermediate Sanctions safe harbor requirements provide that there is a rebuttable presumption of reasonableness that applies to a financial arrangement with any person with substantial influence over an organization if the financial arrangement was approved by an independent board (or an independent committee comprised of board members) that:

  1. Was composed entirely of individuals unrelated to and not subject to the control of the disqualified person(s) involved in the arrangement.

  2. Obtained and relied upon "appropriate data" as to comparability.

     For compensation, data might include compensation levels paid by similarly situated organizations (both tax-exempt and taxable) for functionally comparable positions; the location of the organization, including the availability of similar specialties in the geographic area; current compensation surveys compiled by independent firms; or actual written offers from similar organizations competing for the services of the disqualified person. For property transactions, relevant information includes current independent appraisals and offers received as part of an open and competitive bidding process.

3. Adequately documented the basis for its decision when the actual decision was made.

For example, the board minutes should include the terms of the transaction and date of approval, the members present and voting, the comparability data relied upon and how it was obtained, and any actions taken regarding consideration of the matter by anyone on the board or committee who had a conflict of interest.

PRACTICAL TIPS

✓ In addition to paying close attention to the legal requirements for setting appropriate compensation, be sensitive to the public's perception of what is acceptable or reasonable.

✓ Do your homework: There are numerous national and local nonprofit compensation surveys available.

✓ For smaller nonprofits that can't afford costly consultants or published national surveys, do local research and investigate compensation packages in similar organizations. Contact the organizations directly or rely on GuideStar for posted Form 990s.

✓ Equally, when financial benefits must be limited, there are many other ways the board can compensate and support the chief executive. Consider a more flexible working environment, opportunities for professional development, and sabbaticals.

✓ Many of the above-mentioned guidelines should be considered when reviewing compensation of other executive staff, particularly the chief operating officer, chief financial officer, and anyone else with substantial influence over the organization or a major section of the organization.

SAMPLE EXECUTIVE COMPENSATION POLICIES

The three policies included range from very simple to very specific. Generally speaking, the more complex the organization and the more money at stake, the more explicit the compensation policy should be.

1. This simple policy delegates responsibility for managing the performance review and compensation determination process to a committee that will work with an external consultant.

2. This comprehensive policy, most suited to larger, more complex institutions (in this case, a university), delegates authority, specifies responsibilities, and outlines a process for determining executive compensation.

3. This sample outlines the organization's compensation philosophy and acceptable sources for comparable pay.

SUGGESTED RESOURCES

- Hryvna, Mark. "NPT Salary Survey 2006: Women Catching Up with Men, but Neither With Inflation." *The NonProfit Times.* February, 2006.

- Lipman, Harvey. "Few Organizations Have Policies to Guide Decisions on Compensation." *The Chronicle of Philanthropy.* November, 2005.

- McLaughlin, Thomas A. "Executive Compensation: Measuring What Is Fair and Reasonable." *The NonProfit Times.* August 1, 2003.

- Miller, Steven T. "Rebuttable Presumption Procedure is Key to Easy Intermediate Sanctions Compliance." www.irs.gov/pub/irs-tege/m4958a2.pdf

- "Recommended Best Practices in Determining Reasonable Executive Compensation." Council on Foundations. December 6, 2002. www.cof.org/files/Documents/Governing_Boards/execcomp2003.pdf

- Vogel, Brian H. and Charles W. Quatt. *Dollars and Sense: The Nonprofit Board's Guide to Determining Chief Executive Compensation.* Washington, DC: BoardSource, 2005.

4. EXECUTIVE TRANSITION

INTRODUCTION

The search for a new chief executive is an extraordinary opportunity for a board to have a lasting impact on the growth and success of the organization it governs. One of the most concrete performance indicators for a governing board is the quality of the chief executive recruited and retained by the board. All too often, however, board members underplan and underinvest in this critical task. While it is often impossible to plan every step of an executive transition in advance, a board with an established policy and a regular succession planning process will be better prepared to handle the task when it arises.

KEY ELEMENTS

- Executive transitions are normal and inevitable, so the real test is in how they are handled. Chief executives may leave unexpectedly or after a duly announced resignation, or they may be let go before the previously agreed tenure is over. Without any succession planning, the board is in the precarious position of having to manage the transition with limited information.

- The board needs an emergency transition plan to help it move forward quickly when an unexpected loss of a chief executive takes place. This does not mean that a successor is named ahead of time but that the process for handling the transition period is clear and in place.

- Long-term succession plan ingredients include organizational evaluation, the need to define the qualifications and special skills for a new chief executive, and an adjustment of the job description accordingly.

PRACTICAL TIPS

✓ Involve the current chief executive in succession planning, which will help take the secrecy out of the situation. Work with the chief executive to ensure that the organization has up-to-date operating manuals and appropriate archives. When possible, engage the chief executive in creating resources and plans to help with transition. One important aspect of preparing for succession is for the chief executive to keep the board informed about his or her own future plans.

✓ Develop a public relations plan for notifying key constituencies and the public about the transition.

SAMPLE EXECUTIVE TRANSITION POLICIES

The sample policies address preparedness for the eventual loss of the chief executive and assign transition teams to carry on the activities.

1. This simple policy serves as a reminder to the board of its responsibility for executive succession planning.

2. This brief sample gives the board chair the power to form a search committee.

3. This policy requires the chief executive to identify other executives who are capable of carrying out critical duties in the event of an emergency.

4. This sample incorporates succession planning into the annual performance review and assigns responsibility to both the executive committee and the chief executive.

SUGGESTED RESOURCES

- Axelrod, Nancy R. *Chief Executive Succession Planning: The Board's Role in Securing Your Organization's Future*. Washington, DC: BoardSource, 2002.

- Bell, Jeanne, Richard Moyers, and Timothy Wolfred. "Daring to Lead 2006: A National Study of Nonprofit Executive Leadership." CompassPoint and The Meyer Foundation, 2006. www.compasspoint.org/assets/ 194_daringtolead06final.pdf

- "Capturing the Power of Leadership Change: Using Executive Transition Management to Strengthen Organizational Capacity." Baltimore, MD: The Annie E. Casey Foundation, 2004.

- Tierney, Thomas J. "The Nonprofit Sector's Leadership Deficit." *Bridgespan Group*. Summer 2006.

Part IV: Finance and Investments

1. Budgeting

2. Capital Expenditures

3. Financial Controls

4. Investments

5. Reserves and Endowments

6. Financial Audits

7. IRS Form 990 and 990-PF

8. Risk Management

1. BUDGETING

INTRODUCTION

Every responsible organization needs a budget. A budget is a planning document that forecasts expected revenue and expenses for the coming year. The master budget reflects financial activities for the entire organization, and it is a compilation of individual department and project budgets. A budget policy recognizes the importance of this annual process and ensures that the staff and the board remain accountable for their roles in financial planning and oversight.

KEY ELEMENTS

- Preparing the budget is a staff responsibility, but the board needs to approve the final document. The board or finance committee (see Part VIII: Committees, Section 2: Financial Committees) should also monitor how well the budget has been implemented by tracking performance (e.g., financial reports) on a regular basis and reviewing and approving any midyear adjustments.

- A budget policy should outline the timeline and review process for budgeting, ensuring that the appropriate staff and board committees are involved before the final board approval.

- A budget policy may specify additional details for expected percentage of cost increases, assumptions for calculating revenue and expenses, or desired surplus levels.

PRACTICAL TIPS

- ✓ The budget policy outlines the responsibilities for different parts of the budgeting process. Use it as a reminder to recruit board members and staff with the necessary financial skills and business planning acumen.

- ✓ Review the budget policy regularly. As the financial situation and maturity of the organization evolves, so does the complexity of the budgeting process.

- ✓ A budget is not a public document; it is an internal planning document. Consider stating in the policy whether the budget can be shared with outsiders.

SAMPLE BUDGETING POLICIES

The sample budgeting policies included vary from outlining respective responsibilities during the budgeting process to providing more detail to guide staff in resource allocation.

1. This policy clarifies that once the budget is approved, it is the chief executive's responsibility to manage within those terms.

2. This sample provides parameters within which the chief executive must work when developing the budget.

3. This policy states the purpose of the budgeting process and addresses preparation, approval, and review.

SUGGESTED RESOURCES

- Blazek, Jody. *Financial Planning for Nonprofit Organizations.* New York: John Wiley & Sons, 2000.

- Dropkin, Murray and Bill LaTouche. *The Budget-Building Book for Nonprofits: A Step-by-Step Guide for Managers and Boards.* New York: John Wiley & Sons, 2005.

- McLaughlin, Thomas A. *Presenting: Nonprofit Financials.* Washington, DC: BoardSource, 2001.

2. CAPITAL EXPENDITURES

INTRODUCTION

A capital expenditure is money spent on acquiring or upgrading physical assets of the organization, such as buildings, real estate, furniture, and equipment. Accounting rules define how such expenses may be depreciated. Some small nonprofits prepare their financial statement on the cash basis. In these cases, fixed assets are neither capitalized nor depreciated. However, procedures should still be in place pertaining to financial controls and approvals of capital items. Because many capital expenditures represent a significant investment and considerable cash outlay, nonprofit boards often establish financial limits beyond which a chief executive cannot go without board approval.

KEY ELEMENTS

- The board should define the level of spending that constitutes a capital expenditure and any approval processes. These should govern routine expenses, such as office equipment, computer upgrades, and building maintenance.

- Expenditure policies should define the useful life of different types of assets and whether depreciation is budgeted or not budgeted from the funds used for capital expenditures.

PRACTICAL TIPS

✓ When creating a capital expenditure policy, clarify the difference between operating expenditures and long-term expenditures. A capital item has a useful life of more than a year. Operating items are consumed or used up within one year.

✓ When an organization undertakes a major, planned investment, such as building a new facility, the board should consider establishing special policies to guide these out-of-the-ordinary capital expenditures.

✓ Because capital expenditures are generally large investments, the board and staff should work together on creating a multiyear capital financial forecast. This will help plan ahead for major cash outlays, such as Web designs, accounting software, and office expansions.

✓ Consider establishing a separate sinking fund or capital improvement fund savings account for physical assets; the policy should clarify how and when it can be used.

SAMPLE CAPITAL EXPENDITURE POLICIES

The samples provide guidelines for boards in their oversight of capital expenditures.

1. This policy defines capital expenditures and provides guidelines related to budgeting and purchasing procedures.

2. This policy emphasizes different approval authority depending on the nature of the capital expenditure.

SUGGESTED RESOURCES

*   Dropkin, Murray and Bill LaTouche. *The Budget-Building Book for Nonprofits: A Step-by-Step Guide for Managers and Boards.* New York: John Wiley & Sons, 2005.

*   McLaughlin, Thomas A. *Presenting: Nonprofit Financials.* Washington, DC: BoardSource, 2001.

*   Stevens, Susan Kenny. *All the Way to the Bank: Smart Nonprofit Money Management.* Minneapolis, MN: LarsonAllen Public Service Group, 2002.

3. FINANCIAL CONTROLS

INTRODUCTION

As part of its financial oversight of the organization, the board is responsible for ensuring that appropriate internal controls are in place — and adhered to — to protect the organization. These internal controls ensure that the organization is using generally accepted accounting principles, complying with applicable laws and regulations, providing reliable financial information, and operating efficiently. More specifically, financial controls are designed to segregate financial duties, protect against asset loss, protect cash receipts, require second signatures on large checks, keep track of inventory, require an efficient bidding process, produce timely reports, and maintain accurate record keeping.

KEY ELEMENTS

*   Good financial practice requires boards to have policies for the handling of money by staff and board alike. Such policies include controls put on

check-signing authority, transfer of funds, cash disbursement, and other financial transactions.

- Financial controls provide broad guidelines for significant financial transactions, but the board should not get involved in determining (or monitoring) how the staff handles daily transactions.

- An area of financial concern is the approval of capital expenditures (see Part IV: Finance and Investments, Section 2: Capital Expenditures), such as for equipment and other tangible assets, made by the staff. Nonprofit organizations often have financial limits beyond which a chief executive cannot go without board approval.

Practical Tips

✓ Depending on the scope of the organization's other financial policies, consider requiring that certain internal management controls be established and reviewed annually.

✓ In managing funds, the board generally delegates day-to-day control to staff; however, the board should keep control of borrowing money. Excessive borrowing is not in the interest of the organization and may signal a lack of sufficient financial controls on the part of staff and board.

✓ Review the organization's financial policies and procedures regularly. This task can be delegated to the audit or finance committee (see Part VIII: Committees, Section 2: Financial Committees).

✓ If the board approves the establishment of credit card accounts for the organization, the chief executive must set clear processes to ensure proper use of the cards for business purposes only.

Sample Financial Control Policies

If the organization does not have a single, all-encompassing financial policy, the board should ensure that some specific polices are instituted. The samples address a variety of different issues, and they are offered as examples of common internal control policies.

1. This brief policy establishes general guidelines for financial controls and clarifies what requires board approval.

2. This short and simple policy provides basic requirements for check signing and cash disbursements.

3. This short policy covers check signing, withdrawal of funds, and deposits, and requires the check signers to be bonded.

4. This sample provides criteria and guidelines should the organization need to borrow funds or establish a line of credit.

5. Generally, nonprofits do not make loans to board or staff members because they are usually prohibited by state nonprofit corporation statutes and because they may cause "excess benefit transactions." This policy provides stringent guidelines for those rare instances when they are allowed and appropriate.

6. Through this policy, the board authorizes the chief executive to define processes for credit cards for business use. However, the board should retain the authority to set appropriate credit limits.

7. Because corporate credit cards can complicate accounting procedures and are ripe for abuse, some organizations choose not to use them. This policy allows for a single corporate card to be used only in emergency situations.

8. This brief statement connects the organization's purchasing activities to its values related to diversity and community service.

SUGGESTED RESOURCES

- American Bar Association Coordinating Committee. *Guide to Nonprofit Corporate Governance in the Wake of Sarbanes-Oxley*. Chicago, IL: American Bar Association, 2005.

- Berger, Steven. *Understanding Nonprofit Financial Statements*. Washington, DC: BoardSource, 2003.

- Gross, Malvern J., Jr., John H. McCarthy, and Nancy E. Shelmon. *Financial and Accounting Guide for Not-for-Profit Organizations, 7th ed.* New York: John Wiley & Sons, 2005.

- Lang, Andrew S. *Financial Responsibilities of Nonprofit Boards*. Washington, DC: BoardSource, 2003.

4. INVESTMENTS

INTRODUCTION

Wise investing provides an opportunity to increase revenues and decrease pressure on fundraising and other sources of revenue. Any organization that has assets to invest should also have appropriate policies to safeguard those investments. Such policies can range from simple introductory statements to complex details useful only to the most sophisticated investment committees.

KEY ELEMENTS

- A basic investment policy identifies the assets available for investing, defines general investment objectives, sets asset allocation parameters (e.g., diversification), and clarifies the organization's tolerance for risk (by defining required ratings).

- Investment policies are not only for large organizations with considerable endowments. A responsible board makes sure that policies exist to get the best return from any cash surplus. Likewise, investment policies are reviewed and revised as the organization grows.

- An investment policy often defines the role of an investment manager in day-to-day management of the funds, specifies his or her accountability (e.g., risk in transactions, reporting requirements, and coverage of cash flow needs), and designates a board committee (see Part VIII: Committees, Section 2: Financial Committees) or the full board to monitor the manager's performance and that of the portfolio.

- The investment policy offers some protection from liability. By faithfully adhering to the requirements of the investment policy, the board may reduce the chances of arbitrary or inappropriate investments, and thus limit the viability of any charges that it breached fiduciary duties.

- The Uniform Management of Institutional Funds Act (UMIFA) and the Uniform Prudent Investor Act (UPIA) govern the investment of most nonprofit funds and focus on portfolio performance rather than returns on individual transactions. This gives nonprofits greater flexibility in taking reasonable risks with their investments.

PRACTICAL TIPS

✓ When determining investment goals, take short-term and long-term goals into consideration. The purpose of the specific fund can help determine the priorities — growth, liquidity, or security — and the level of acceptable risk.

✓ When diversifying the portfolio, consider different types of investments (e.g., stocks, bonds, alternative and cash equivalents) in different classes (e.g., corporate vs. U.S. Treasury bonds, and large, medium, or small company stocks) in different industries.

✓ Consider adopting socially responsible investment guidelines, restricting investment activity in liquor, tobacco, arms, and other potentially controversial industries.

SAMPLE INVESTMENT POLICIES

Investment policies provide direction for the nonprofit's board about how accumulated funds should be invested. Some organizations simply need a statement to clarify how any cash surplus is treated, and others require a comprehensive policy defining the purpose and use of a substantial endowment. The sample policies included are arranged in order of increasing specificity.

1. This general policy establishes an investment committee, authorizes retention of an investment consultant, and then addresses all of the standard investment policy issues.

2. Goals and responsibilities are thoroughly defined in this sample. It incorporates social investment as part of its investment goals.

3. This policy defines different categories of funds and their investment objectives, and distinguishes responsibilities between board and staff.

4. This simple policy establishes guidelines for short-term operating reserves and delegates responsibility to the chief executive.

5. This sample addresses other investment assets, such as property and equipment, and clarifies priorities in each fund.

6. This comprehensive investment policy addresses the unique needs of a foundation and includes signature lines for the foundation and investment manager.

SUGGESTED RESOURCES

- Fry, Robert P. *Minding the Money: An Investment Guide for Nonprofit Board Members*. Washington, DC: BoardSource, 2004.

- Panel on the Nonprofit Sector: www.nonprofitpanel.org/supplemental/ 1_Prudent_Investor.pdf

- "Prudent Investment Practices: An Overview." *Association of Small Foundations Quarterly Newsletter*. Winter 2005.

- Schneider, William A., Robert A. DiMeo, and Michael S. Benoit. *The Practical Guide to Managing Nonprofit Assets*. New York: John Wiley & Sons, 2005.

5. RESERVES AND ENDOWMENTS

INTRODUCTION

Financial reserves act as a safeguard for rainy days and permit an organization to adjust to seasonal variances in expenses and income. Market forces, economic downturns, natural disasters, or other unexpected expenses cannot be controlled by nonprofit managers, but expenses related to them can — and should — be managed. Reserve funds allow an organization to continue activity when income falls unexpectedly, such as when clients are unable to pay their bills on time, when contributions decline substantially, or when a significant grant is not realized. These funds also allow an organization to seize an unprecedented opportunity, such as financing a new venture, making an advantageous capital purchase, or expanding a program at an opportune time.

Reserve funds usually come from the accumulated surpluses of the organization over time. The board, with input from staff, should establish a reserve policy that maintains an appropriate level for the organization, given its mission. Reserve funds are usually designated or allocated by the board as a way to ensure the long-term financial stability of the organization.

Many nonprofit organizations — besides accumulating operational reserves — have established or wish to establish an endowment fund. Endowment funds are generally maintained so that the principal is continually invested and the withdrawals (usually a percentage of the endowment's market value) are used by the organization for program expenses. However, there can be pressure on organizations to invade the principal or dissolve the fund in periods of financial stress. Policies are needed to guide the board in making decisions about the endowment — how it should be invested and how it should be used.

KEY ELEMENTS

- The distinction between reserves and endowment is significant. An endowment is a pool of money that is invested so that the income can be used to support the nonprofit. Often, donors have restricted these funds so that the principal cannot be used to cover day-to-day expenses. Reserve funds are more flexible. Reserves usually come from the accumulated surpluses of the organization over time, can be spent to expand programs and run the organization, and are usually designated or allocated by the board.

- Reserve policies state the required reserve level in terms of months of operating cash, meaning that, should all sources of income stop, the organization would be able to keep running for that period of time.

- Board approval is usually required for any disbursements from the reserves fund.

- Establishing an endowment fund requires a special policy that defines its purpose, who manages the fund, the investment approach, and how the money will be disbursed.

- When created by donors, endowment funds are bound by legal agreements. The donors' wishes need to be respected and the money can be used only for the assigned purpose. Even the board may not change the original restrictions on the fund, as it can with operating reserves.

- Generally speaking, private foundations must disburse approximately 5 percent of the value of their endowments annually. Many nonprofits traditionally use the same percentage when determining the disbursement rate for their endowment funds.

PRACTICAL TIPS

- ✓ Responsibility for monitoring the board-designated reserve is often delegated to the finance and/or investment committee.

- ✓ When establishing the level of operating reserves, the board and executive staff need to balance the need for equity that generates future income against immediate operating and cash flow needs.

- ✓ Endowments may be created by special endowment campaigns, major gifts or planned gifts, or by pooling operational reserves into a specified endowment fund. When appropriate for the organization, one useful way to grow an endowment fund is to establish a planned giving program. Consult with your accountants to ensure (when possible) that such endowment funds are board designated, not donor designated.

✓ Gift acceptance policies (see Part V: Fundraising, Section 3: Gift Acceptance) complement endowment policies by providing guidelines for working with the donors. Likewise, consider including specific requirements for endowments in your investment policies (see Part IV: Finance and Investments, Section 4: Investments).

SAMPLE RESERVE AND ENDOWMENT POLICIES

With a policy on operating reserves, the board ensures that the organization is ready to react to unexpected events. By drafting a policy on endowments, the board guarantees that the permanent fund is truly dedicated to the originally intended purpose. The two sample reserve policies are deceptively simple and require careful consideration by an organization's leaders. The three endowment policies provide basic boundaries for endowments.

1. This brief policy provides basic guidelines related to the reserve fund and board approval.

2. This sample operating reserve objective provides a greater level of detail, which can be applied to specific fund objectives. It is for organizations with significant reserves relative to their regular cash flow requirements and illustrates one approach to increasing returns on these funds.

3. This succinct statement defines the basic description and objective of an endowment.

4. This general policy reserves the right, for the board, to dissolve the endowment fund if the purposes can no longer be met.

5. This endowment spending policy includes specific distribution values.

SUGGESTED RESOURCES

- "Endowments," Special section. *The Chronicle of Philanthropy*. May 27–28, 2004.

- Fry, Robert P. *Minding the Money: An Investment Guide for Nonprofit Board Members*. Washington, DC: BoardSource, 2004.

- Larkin, Richard F. "Nonprofits and Squirrels: Or, How Big a Reserve Do You Need?" *The NonProfit Times*. April 1, 2004.

- Schumacher, Edward C. and Timothy L. Seiler. *Building Your Endowment*. San Francisco: Jossey-Bass, 2003.

- Zeitlow, John T., Jo Ann Hankin, and Alan G. Seidner. *Financial Management for Nonprofit Organizations: Policies and Practices*. New York: John Wiley & Sons, 2006.

6. Financial Audits

Introduction

An audit refers to an independent professional examination of the organization's financial statements and its support materials. The audit will attest to the *fair presentation* of the financial statements; it will not guarantee their accuracy. Nonprofit organizations — and their boards — benefit from the annual audit as an outside assessment of their financial status and their internal financial controls, as a tool to improve financial and risk management, and as a measure of assurance to constituents and supporters who want to know that their trust and support is deserved.

Financial audits are recommended for organizations with budgets of $1 million or more. California requires any nonprofit with gross revenues of $2 million or more to conduct an annual audit, and some states have much lower revenue thresholds (e.g., $250,000). Furthermore, most organizations that receive government funding are obligated to have an audit. In weighing the benefits of an audit against the expense, many organizations with smaller budgets choose to have an independent accountant prepare or review their financial statements. If the board decides not to have an annual audit, it may choose to conduct a less comprehensive and costly review or to have the audit take place biennially.

Key Elements

- The auditor reports to the board and assists management. Responsibility for hiring an auditor belongs to the board, and the full board should receive and review the auditor's report, management letter, and the IRS Form 990.

- Some nonprofits, especially larger organizations, have adopted audit practices that mirror those required of publicly traded companies through the Sarbanes-Oxley Act of 2002. They have addressed concerns about auditor independence by requiring rotation of the audit firm or partner periodically, and by stipulating what other professional services the auditor may or may not perform.

- When a board decides that an audit is desirable, it often delegates certain responsibilities to a separate audit committee (see Part VIII: Committees, Section 2: Financial Committees). The role of this committee is to act on behalf of the full board in carrying out the audit process. This committee may also assume oversight of the organization's overall ethical standards.

Practical Tips

✓ Have an executive session with the full board and the auditor, without any staff present. This provides the board with an opportunity to openly review the results of the audit and management letter and to ask candid questions about the organization's financial health without creating unnecessary distrust between the board and senior staff.

- ✓ The auditor is in a good position to provide guidance and expertise concerning internal controls and general financial practices (see Part IV: Finance and Investments, Section 3: Financial Controls). Take advantage of the auditor's presence to learn about current issues in nonprofit accounting and auditing and areas for improvement in the organization's financial systems and structure.

- ✓ Increasingly, nonprofit boards are separating the audit from financial oversight to ensure appropriate checks and balances. If the finance committee also handles the audit, be sure committee members understand the distinction between routine financial review and the annual audit.

- ✓ The auditor also needs support from management to complete the audit. Rather than waiting for the auditor's instructions, the finance staff should organize files and records in advance of the auditor's arrival to save time. The auditor should send a preliminary listing of items needed for an efficient start to the audit.

SAMPLE FINANCIAL AUDIT POLICIES

All three sample audit policies require an annual financial audit. They range from a very simple acknowledgment of the board's responsibility for the audit, to more detailed requirements about the process.

1. This basic policy mandates an annual audit and its distribution.

2. This sample delegates certain responsibilities to the audit committee and requires periodic rotation of the auditors.

3. This more comprehensive policy includes guidelines for selecting the audit firm and monitoring the entire audit process.

SUGGESTED RESOURCES

- American Bar Association Coordinating Committee. *Guide to Nonprofit Corporate Governance in the Wake of Sarbanes-Oxley.* Chicago, IL: American Bar Association, 2005.

- McLaughlin, Thomas A. *Financial Committees.* Washington, DC: BoardSource, 2004.

- Ober|Kaler, attorneys at law. *The Nonprofit Legal Landscape.* BoardSource, 2005.

7. IRS FORM 990 AND 990-PF

INTRODUCTION

The Form 990 or 990-PF is an annual information return that nonprofits file with the IRS. This public document provides information that allows the IRS to determine whether the organization continues to fill the requirements for its tax-exempt status. Every nonprofit (other than a private foundation) with average annual gross receipts (three-year rolling average) of at least $25,000 must file a Form 990 with the IRS annually; every private foundation, regardless of revenue or asset size, must file a Form 990-PF with the IRS. Both annual information returns include an income and expense statement; a functional expense allocation; additional information about the organization's programs, relationships with officers, directors, and key employees; and compliance with the applicable requirements of §501(c).

KEY ELEMENTS

- Form 990 or 990-PF is often filled out by a professional advisor (e.g., accountant or trust officer). Requiring internal verification adds an additional level of accountability. The signature of the chief executive or the chief financial officer serves as a testament to the accuracy of the information.

- Establishing a policy on public disclosure of Form 990 or 990-PF emphasizes the organization's commitment to public transparency and compliance with the law. Subject to minimal exceptions, §6104(d) of the Internal Revenue Code requires all tax-exempt organizations to make their last three Forms 990 or 990-PF available for public inspection, and to provide copies to anyone requesting it in writing. These rules are set out in detail in General Instruction M to Form 990 and General Instruction Q to Form 990-PF.

- Because Form 990 or 990-PF is a public document, it simply makes sense that the governing body of the organization be aware of its contents in advance of disclosure. By creating a policy that requires the board to receive the Form 990 or 990-PF, the organization makes a commitment to internal transparency as well.

PRACTICAL TIPS

- ✓ To ensure that each board member is familiar with the contents of the Form 990 or 990-PF, the chief executive should provide a copy to each board member and have the minutes of a board meeting record that this has happened. Most auditors review the Form 990 or 990-PF in detail with the board during audit committee meetings.

- ✓ Accountability and transparency are keys to retaining public trust, and nonprofits can accomplish it by providing easy and open access to this document. The easiest way to facilitate the availability of the Form 990 or 990-PF is to post a copy on the organization's Web site. Most 990s and 990-PFs are also electronically available through GuideStar (www.guidestar.org).

- ✓ The Forms 990 and 990-PF require that the organization list board members and key staff, their compensation, and their addresses. Rather than using anyone's personal address, use the organization's mailing address or a PO Box.

- ✓ A charity need not publicly disclose the names of donors and the amounts of individual contributions. This information may be listed as an attachment — marked "Not Subject to Public Inspection" — that does not have to be made publicly available. A private foundation must disclose this information, however.

Sample IRS Form 990 and 990-PF Policies

The two samples provided are brief but they include responsibilities of both board and staff in making the appropriate information available to the public.

1. This simple policy articulates expectations related to the Form 990 or 990-PF.

2. This checklist outlines a series of proactive steps that staff undertakes, with board oversight, to publicly disclose financial information, including the Form 990 and audited financial statements.

Suggested Resources

*   Blazek, Jody. *IRS Form 990: Tax Preparation Guide for Nonprofits, Revised.* New York: John Wiley & Sons, 2004.

*   GuideStar: www.guidestar.org

*   IRS Instructions for Form 990 and Form 990-EZ (2005): www.irs.gov/instructions/i990-ez/index.html

*   Ober|Kaler, attorneys at law. *The Nonprofit Legal Landscape.* Washington, DC: BoardSource, 2005.

8. Risk Management

Introduction

One of the board's responsibilities is to safeguard the organization's resources — both human and financial. By putting a risk-management policy in writing, the organization communicates its commitment to managing potential organizational threats. This policy statement reflects the organization's mission and purpose, states the intent of the program, and lists the actions that others throughout the organization can take to contribute to the organization's risk-management efforts.

Key Elements

*   A comprehensive risk-management policy identifies potential risks to the organization, evaluates their prevalence, and selects suitable techniques to deal with them. These techniques may include ways to avoid the risk (fix broken railing), modify its presence (install burglar alarm), accept the possibility for the risk to materialize (low probability for floods), or transfer the consequences to someone else (purchase insurance).

*   For many nonprofits, risk management includes a variety of other policies, such as employee hiring and screening policies, safety and accident reporting policies, investment policies (see Part IV: Finance and Investments, Section 4: Investments), and other personnel-related policies (see Part VI: Personnel).

PRACTICAL TIPS

✓ With respect to the risks posed by the decisions and operations of the board, in addition to purchasing directors' and officers' liability insurance, adopt board policies to address issues like conflict of interest and indemnification (see Part I: Ethics and Accountability, Section 4: Conflict of Interest).

✓ The organization's commitment should go beyond developing a policy statement and having proper insurance policies. Be sure to put a risk-management plan in place. A risk-management plan describes an organization's priority risks and the strategies the organization has identified to prevent harm or loss, or to respond to incidents should prevention measures fail. It helps to protect not only paid and volunteer staff, but also the general public.

SAMPLE RISK-MANAGEMENT POLICIES

A basic risk-management policy is a brief statement, often just a few sentences. Some nonprofits will include additional guidance about insurance, sources of risk, and risk-management plans.

1. This brief, general statement recognizes the importance of risk management and commits the board to ensuring that a risk-management plan is updated annually.

2. This statement identifies general areas of risk that the chief executive is responsible for managing and provides some guidance on the level of protection.

3. This brief policy specifies what kind of insurance protection must be maintained.

4. This policy reflects the organization's commitment to developing an emergency response and recovery plan. The details are naturally very specific to the organization, but the framework should help others prepare their plan.

SUGGESTED RESOURCES

• Herman, Melanie L. et al. *Managing Risk for Nonprofit Organizations: A Comprehensive Guide.* New York: John Wiley & Sons, 2004.

• Ober|Kaler, attorneys at law. *The Nonprofit Legal Landscape.* Washington, DC: BoardSource, 2005.

• The Nonprofit Risk Management Center: www.nonprofitrisk.org

Part V: Fundraising

1. Board Member Fundraising
2. Donor Relations
3. Gift Acceptance
4. Sponsorships and Endorsements

1. Board Member Fundraising

Introduction

Board members have a crucial role to play in raising funds for the organization they serve. They are volunteers dedicated to the mission of the organization and the people served by the organization. And, they have contacts in the community. The expectation of board member involvement in fundraising continues to rise, yet many boards have not created a policy that specifies what that involvement should entail. A board fundraising policy can take the form of a narrative or a specialized agreement or contract in which board members indicate the amount they expect to contribute to the organization in the coming year and how they will participate in the fundraising efforts of the organization.

Key Elements

- Personal giving policies state whether a board member is expected to give a certain amount or to give according to his or her means. Funders often ask if 100 percent of board members give.

- Fundraising policies establish expectations for board members to make a personal donation and to participate in solicitation efforts. The policy may list examples of how board members can or should be involved, such as providing names of potential donors, writing or signing fundraising letters, thanking donors personally, accompanying the chief executive on donor and foundation visits, or making the ask themselves.

- Some organizations use a special pledge form that guides board members in thinking about the array of fundraising activities taking place throughout the year and asks them to make an annual fundraising commitment.

- Some nonprofits incorporate board member fundraising expectations into more general job descriptions (see Part II: Board and Board Members, Section 1: Role of the Board, and Section 2: Board Member Agreements).

- If the organization has a separate fundraising body (which may be a supporting organization), it is still important to outline the role for board members and how they relate to this body — and vice versa.

Practical Tips

✓ To become a committed fundraiser, a board member must first make a contribution. This requirement is the cornerstone of individual fundraising because it allows a board member to use himself or herself as an example of someone who supports the organization.

✓ Not every board member will be able to give the same size gift. Some organizations stipulate a minimum gift amount; many do not. The policy should encourage each board member to make the organization a priority in his or her personal giving plan or to make what, for that person, is a substantial financial contribution. The policy should not, however, eliminate capable and valuable individuals from joining the board and contributing other skills and expertise.

✓ Board members possess different skill levels and aptitudes for solicitation. Give board members training in fundraising and practical tools like checklists, sample elevator speeches, and steps for approaching a potential donor, to help each member gradually assume more responsibility. Providing mentors and coupling inexperienced board members with staff or more seasoned board members is another way to increase everybody's comfort with personal solicitations.

✓ Some individuals, because of their profession or position (e.g., journalists, judges), may be prohibited from certain kinds of fundraising solicitations (e.g., workplace campaigns). Seek other activities so these board members can still support the organization in a meaningful way.

SAMPLE BOARD MEMBER FUNDRAISING POLICIES

The sample fundraising policies included range from broad statements of general expectations to specific requirements and commitments for board member participation. They are arranged in order of least to most specific.

1. This brief statement acknowledges that each board member should give according to his or her means and should participate in all fundraising efforts.

2. This general policy outlines expectations for board member participation that is beyond simply "giving and getting."

3. This brief sample, which may be incorporated into other statements, identifies a specific sum each board member is responsible for either raising or contributing.

4. This brief statement not only establishes a minimum amount for personal contributions but also separates fundraising obligations from personal giving.

5. This sample statement suggests more personal ways that board members can support the organization's fundraising activities. It was adapted from a national organization to encourage board members to get involved in local fundraising.

6. This statement summarizes how board members are expected to actively participate in fundraising. It refers to three major areas of responsibility in this regard — leadership, personal action, and advocacy — and is also meant to be used as a guide to evaluate board members' performance in fundraising.

7. This more comprehensive sample, in the form of an annual pledge, specifies the level of contribution, level of participation in fundraising activities, and ability to donate or identify in-kind giving sources. This form needs to be prefaced by an explanation in the job description for new board members in order for them to feel comfortable with this expectation.

Suggested Resources

- George, Worth. *Fearless Fundraising for Nonprofit Boards*. Washington, DC: BoardSource, 2003.

- Greenfield, James M. *Fundraising Responsibilities of Nonprofit Boards*. Washington, DC: BoardSource, 2003.

- *Speaking of Money*. Video or DVD with 15-page user's guide. Washington, DC: BoardSource, 1996.

- Weisman, Carol. *Secrets of Successful Fundraising*. St. Louis, MO: F.E. Robbins & Sons Press, 2000.

2. Donor Relations

Introduction

Treating donors with respect, gratitude, and consideration not only makes sense but is also the only way a charitable organization will keep donors coming back. A nonprofit organization is accountable to the public *and* to the donors who support it. Respecting donors' wishes, first and foremost, demonstrates responsible and ethical behavior. If a donor makes an unrestricted contribution, the organization is free to use the money to advance the mission however it deems appropriate. If a donor specifies what the money is to be used for or puts conditions on the contribution, the organization is obligated to follow the donor's wishes if it accepts the gift. Donors have a right to know that their contributions have been put to good use.

Key Elements

- Recognizing donors for their gifts is an essential part of responsible fundraising. There are numerous ways this can be done, but it is best managed by clear guidelines that spell out the process and define the levels and methods of recognition.

- A donor relations policy should be clear about proper handling of confidentiality and anonymity desired by some donors. Additional guidelines should state how to treat donor contact information and how the donor prefers to be listed or named in recognition vehicles.

- Federal tax law imposes rules as to written substantiation of contributions above specific amounts and statements as to whether a donor has received anything in return that might lower the deductible portion of the contribution.

Practical Tips

- ✓ Following rules of accounting on how to record unrestricted, temporarily restricted, and restricted grants and donations is the only way to keep track of the use of donated funds.

- ✓ Always keep the donor informed. He or she has the right to know how his or her contribution or grant is being used and what the organization has been able to accomplish with the gift. In the policy, stipulate what information is shared with donors and at what intervals.

- ✓ Donor intent must be honored. If conditions change and the donor's intent can no longer be followed, go back to the donor (if possible) and negotiate another use for the balance of the funds. It is best to do this as soon as it becomes clear that the funds will need to be reallocated or the term of the grant extended. It is inadvisable to wait for the formal grant reporting deadline.

- ✓ When defining the different levels of recognition, always leave the options open for a major gift. It is desirable to be able to provide a worthy and equitable recognition for the gift.

- ✓ Share with all major donors your audited financial statements and annual reports.

- ✓ Adopt the Donor Bill of Rights as a way to let donors know that their needs are respected in the organization. (A copy of the Donor Bill of Rights is included at the end of the sample donor relations policies.)

SAMPLE DONOR RELATIONS POLICIES

The first two samples provided are policies related to donor recognition and informing donors appropriately. The third sample is the Donor Bill of Rights, which is a good addition to (not a substitute for) a donor relations policy.

1. This succinct policy highlights some of the key elements in donor recognition.

2. This policy includes more specifics about the information provided to donors.

3. The Donor Bill of Rights was created by the Giving Institute: Leading Consultants to Non-Profits [formerly known as the American Association of Fund Raising Counsel (AAFRC)], Association for Healthcare Philanthropy (AHP), the Association of Fundraising Professionals (AFP), and the Council for Advancement and Support of Education (CASE). It has been endorsed by numerous other nonprofit associations, and many charities incorporate it into their operating policies and procedures.

SUGGESTED RESOURCES

- • Tempel, Eugene R., ed. *Understanding Donor Dynamics: The Organizational Side of Charitable Giving: New Directions for Philanthropic Fundraising, No. 32.* San Francisco: Jossey-Bass, 2002.

- • *The Donor Bill of Rights:* www.case.org/Content/AboutCASE/ Display.cfm?CONTENTITEMID=2569

3. GIFT ACCEPTANCE

INTRODUCTION

Nearly all charitable organizations accept, and most actively solicit, financial gifts. However, there are times when the perception of such gifts might compromise the mission of the organization or the gift might have too many conditions imposed by the donor. Having a gift acceptance policy helps the board decide whether to accept controversial gifts. Because nonprofits also receive non-cash contributions, clear gift acceptance policies provide guidance as to whether the organization should accept gifts of real estate, stock, art, or automobiles, and how those gifts will be liquidated or maintained.

KEY ELEMENTS

- A nonprofit organization need not accept a gift simply because it is offered. A gift acceptance policy defines the types of gifts the organization will allow.

- Not every gift is a blessing. Donors and nonprofits don't always share the same values and priorities. Gifts that do not enhance the organization's mission, priorities, and reputation should not be accepted.

- Planned giving vehicles, such as bequests and charitable trusts, require that the organization have the capacity to administer them. They may not be appropriate for every organization.

PRACTICAL TIPS

- ✓ The federal law mandates how certain kinds of gifts (e.g., cars, real estate, art) must be documented, valued, and even taxed. Work with lawyers specialized in charitable giving to avoid problems for the organization, and ask that donors do the same.

- ✓ To protect the organization's integrity, consider having a policy that requires the immediate sale of gifts of securities. This eliminates ethical concerns about affiliation with certain companies and avoids second guessing the timing of stock sales.

- ✓ Remain true to the beliefs and values of the organization and do not allow a major donor to lead you off course or to compromise your objectives.

- ✓ Seek ways to encourage donors to make unrestricted gifts that support the general operating budget. Donor restrictions and conditions must be acceptable to the organization and not endanger the tax deductibility of the contribution. Negotiating with generous but demanding donors may be time consuming, but it is important that both parties agree on the terms of the gift and that the gift reflects an investment in programs that advance the mission of the organization.

✓ Seriously consider whether the nature of the gift or the source of the gift is in conflict with the mission of your organization. For example, should an environmental organization accept funding from a known environmental offender, or should a gun control advocacy organization accept funding from an arms manufacturer?

SAMPLE GIFT ACCEPTANCE POLICIES

The sample gift acceptance policies range from a very simple acknowledgment of the board's role in accepting gifts to expansive policies that address values, process, and administrative details. They are arranged in order from least to most comprehensive.

1. This brief policy clarifies the board's right, on behalf of the organization, to refuse a gift.

2. This brief policy specifies how the organization will treat gifts of stock.

3. This short sample establishes the board's role in accepting gifts of property valued over a certain amount.

4. This general policy outlines the basic parameters a nonprofit board and organization should take into account when deciding whether to accept a gift.

5. This policy lists clearly the kinds of gifts that the organization will not accept.

6. This comprehensive sample provides detailed guidance for staff in working with major donors and articulates their respective responsibilities.

7. This comprehensive policy outline presents a thorough gift acceptance policy that addresses ethical considerations, legal requirements, and administrative procedures.

SUGGESTED RESOURCES

- Ford, Robert. "Non-Cash Gifts." *The NonProfit Times Direct Response Fundraising Edition.* March 15, 2005.

- Fraint, Eric. "In-Kind Contributions: How to Account for Them Correctly." *Don Kramer's Nonprofit Issues.* February 16–28, 2005.

- Jordan, Ronald R. and Katelyn L. Quynn. *Planned Giving for Small Nonprofits.* New York: John Wiley & Sons, 2002.

- Tempel, Eugene R. *Development Committee.* Washington, DC: BoardSource, 2004.

4. SPONSORSHIPS AND ENDORSEMENTS

INTRODUCTION

A corporate sponsorship is a financial relationship between a nonprofit organization and a commercial enterprise that is of mutual benefit. In exchange for money, products, or services, the nonprofit provides the corporation with recognition and, at times, use of its name in corporate marketing. Generally, there are four types of corporate sponsorship:

1. Event Marketing: A company sponsors a specific event. For example, Adidas, Heineken, and Hyundai have been sponsors of past Olympic Games.

2. Partner Sponsorship: A long-term partnership between a nonprofit and a corporation. For example, a local mechanic sponsors a little league baseball team.

3. Cause-Related Marketing: A corporate sponsor promotes a specific cause by donating a percentage of its profits from the purchase of a product or service. For example, American Express gives a percentage of its profits to Share Our Strength.

4. Endorsements: A corporation pays a royalty fee for the use of a charity's name or logo on its products. For example, Nicoderm gives money to the American Lung Association to use the ALA name and logo in commercials and on its packaging.

KEY ELEMENTS

- A sponsorship policy defines the relationship between the nonprofit organization and its corporate sponsors. It should provide guidelines on the types of companies the organization will work with and any potential concerns related to the nonprofit's mission and values.

- Sponsorships, by their very nature, require giving the company prominent recognition. A sponsorship policy should establish guidelines for corporate recognition based on the level or value of the sponsorship and, likewise, boundaries for use of the nonprofit's name and logo.

- The policy should also acknowledge who has authority for making sponsorship decisions. Depending on the scale and scope of the organization or the activity, the board may reserve the right to review and even approve corporate sponsorships.

- The board should establish and approve the organization's sponsorship policies, but staff will often handle operational issues, such as negotiating contracts, coordinating communication efforts, and implementing the activities. The board should establish parameters for sponsorship agreements that address limitations and exclusivity, requirements for entering and terminating contracts, and other basic terms.

- Responsibility for corporate sponsorships can be confusing. In nonprofit organizations, either the development or the marketing department may take charge. In corporations, it is often part of the marketing department, rather than the philanthropic or community affairs department.

- Not every nonprofit organization is suited to corporate sponsorships. Small nonprofit organizations may find sponsorship difficult because they lack the staff and resources required to work with a large company. Other organizations, with strong ideology or controversial missions, will find few companies willing to promote their cause.

PRACTICAL TIPS

✓ Engage in the necessary due diligence with respect to a corporation. Make sure that the company's activities, affiliations, business practices, and reputation do not compromise the organization's mission or brand. Ensure that the nonprofit's supporters and stakeholders will be comfortable with this relationship.

✓ Clarify expectations on both sides. What does the organization want out of this relationship? How important is it in the short- and long-term? How does the company want to be recognized? Does it want sole sponsorship?

✓ Remain true to the values of the organization. Do not allow a donor or a sponsor to steer the organization off of its course or beliefs.

✓ Beware of IRS regulations. The IRS regulates sponsorship relationships and separates them from taxable business activities, such as advertising. To avoid taxable income, sponsorship payments should not provide a substantial benefit to the company, but recognition is allowed. You can avoid taxable income and still acknowledge sponsors by citing the sponsor's name, logo, phone number, and address; using value-neutral descriptions of products and services; and linking to the sponsor's Web site's home page.

SAMPLE SPONSORSHIP AND ENDORSEMENT POLICIES

Because there are so many variations on corporate sponsorships, from high-profile events and program underwriting to cobranding and product endorsements, the policies included are relatively general.

1. This succinct statement affirms the organization's commitment to its values and establishes the board's authority for making decisions related to endorsements.

2. This policy encourages active solicitation of sponsors for the organization's programs.

3. This sample provides general guidelines for choosing a sponsor.

4. This policy gives guidelines for product endorsement and sponsorships for special events.

5. This comprehensive policy defines terms, scope, and restrictions for sponsorship activities and clarifies the process for approving contracts.

6. This detailed sample is attentive to the legal definitions of sponsorship and advertising. It details the types of sponsorship and advertising the organization deems acceptable and unacceptable.

SUGGESTED RESOURCES

- Daw, Jocelyne. *Cause Marketing for Nonprofits: Partner for Purpose, Passion, and Profits.* New York: John Wiley & Sons, 2006.

- "How can I find sponsors for an event?" The Nonprofit FAQ. www.idealist.org/if/idealist/en/FAQ/QuestionViewer/default?section=17&item=28

- IRS final regulations: http://frwebgate.access.gpo.gov/cgi-bin/ getdoc.cgi?dbname=2002_register&docid=02-9930-filed.pdf

- Raffa, Thomas J. "Corporate Sponsorship: Acknowledgement or Advertising?" *The Nonprofit Quarterly.* Winter 1999.

Part VI: Personnel

1. RESPONSIBILITY FOR HUMAN RESOURCES

INTRODUCTION

The board is ultimately responsible for the personnel policies of the organization. In practice, this means that the board should periodically review the personnel policies to ensure that they are appropriate and up-to-date. The board may also consider overarching employment policies that reflect the organization's values and desired interactions with its stakeholders — clients, volunteers, staff, and/or the public. That said, except for its supervision of the chief executive, the board does not usually get involved with human resource management. In practice, this means that the board delegates general responsibility to the chief executive for the nonprofit's employment practices.

Personnel policies cover such things as hours of work, paid holidays, paid leave for illness and personal reasons, and employment status. They also cover issues that may lead to litigation, such as employee complaints, discrimination, and sexual harassment. It is especially important for the board to provide guidance on these latter areas. So, in delegating responsibility to the chief executive, the board should be sure to articulate core elements related to human resource issues and the workplace environment.

KEY ELEMENTS

- A simple policy helps to delegate responsibility for the organization's employment practices and procedures to the chief executive. The chief executive, in turn, may carry out that responsibility himself or herself or by assigning it to another employee (e.g., a human resource manager).

- Nonprofit organizations often borrow personnel policies — from more established organizations and/or those with similar programs — to serve as guidelines, but the personnel policies of each organization should reflect the values of that particular organization. The board should ensure that any borrowed policies meet the requirements of the state laws that are applicable to them.

- In young nonprofit organizations, with their first paid staff, the board may be reluctant to create personnel policies out of fear that the policies imply a lack of trust. While board members may want to maintain the collegial work environment, they should not underestimate the value of clear guidelines in helping the organization function better and avoiding potential problems in the future.

PRACTICAL TIPS

- ✓ Make certain that the dissemination of policies to employees does not constitute a contract between management and employees that could result in legal liability under state laws if the policies are not followed. In states where policy manuals may be deemed to constitute contracts, employers can protect themselves by adding a waiver in prominent language, preferably at the beginning of the manual, which states that the manual and/or the policies stated in it do not constitute a contract. Often, this waiver clarifies that employment with the organization is at will, meaning that employees can be terminated for any reason that does not violate federal or state law.

✓ Be sure to have specialists in human resource management and employment law review all personnel policies to make sure they are fair and equitable and that they include all legally required elements. Sometimes, a board member with special expertise may serve as a resource for reviewing and updating the policies.

SAMPLE HUMAN RESOURCE RESPONSIBILITY POLICIES

The two policies provided delegate overall responsibility for employment policies and practices to the chief executive: the first by establishing a positive framework, and the second by defining the minimum requirements.

1. This brief, affirmative statement sets the framework for the organization's employee philosophy and assigns responsibility for personnel policies to the chief executive.

2. This policy defines the management boundaries within which the chief executive must operate vis-à-vis employees and personnel policies.

SUGGESTED RESOURCES

- Barbeito, Carol L. *Human Resource Policies and Procedures for Nonprofit Organizations.* San Francisco: Jossey-Bass, 2006.

- Bernstein, Leyna. *Creating Your Employee Handbook: A Do-It-Yourself Kit for Nonprofits.* San Francisco: Jossey-Bass, 1999.

- Ober|Kaler, attorneys at law. *The Nonprofit Legal Landscape.* Washington, DC: BoardSource, 2005.

- Society for Human Resource Management: www.shrm.org

- U.S. Department of Labor, Occupational Safety & Health Administration: www.osha.gov

2. EQUAL EMPLOYMENT OPPORTUNITY

INTRODUCTION

The most frequent legal actions against nonprofit organizations are in employment areas such as wrongful termination, discrimination, and sexual harassment. It is crucial for nonprofit boards to be vigilant about having nondiscrimination and anti-harassment policies and to see that staff carry them out appropriately.

KEY ELEMENTS

- Discrimination in employment based on race, color, gender, national origin, ethnic background, religion, age, sexual orientation (in some state and local jurisdictions), and disability is illegal, and an organization's policies must be clear about this.

- Equal employment opportunity policies are generally meant to cover the hiring, promotion, job assignments, development, and termination of staff.

- As part of its equal opportunity policy, the organization should also define a complaint process so that employees can speak when they feel that the organization is not treating them fairly or equally (see Part VI: Personnel, Section 6: Complaints).

- Policies related to equal opportunity may be found in several places, ranging from the employee handbook or a code of ethics, to board policies or even bylaws.

PRACTICAL TIPS

- ✓ When crafting equal employment opportunity policies, consider emphasizing proactive efforts alongside the legal requirements. (Employers must be careful to avoid quotas. These are illegal unless the employer has a demonstrated history of illegal discrimination.) The value in equality policies lies in their implementation and in the results they produce. This may require proactive efforts, from training to monitoring to outreach. For example, to broaden the pool of employee applicants, ask staff to scrutinize where they advertise. To assure nondiscrimination in the workplace, offer diversity training.

- ✓ To truly live up to your equal opportunity policies, ensure that you also implement the principles when seeking bids from vendors, recruiting members, or providing services to your customers.

SAMPLE EQUAL EMPLOYMENT OPPORTUNITY POLICIES

The set of policies provided includes basic nondiscrimination policies for employment situations. Some closely mirror the law, while others have more expansive categories and organizational procedures for employee complaints.

1. This short statement fits well within a code of ethics, and lays the foundation for equal employment opportunity.

2. This policy relies on federal nondiscrimination laws as the basis for its employment practices and establishes an Equal Employment Opportunity Commission officer to handle complaints.

3. This document expands the list of protected individuals beyond those required by law, and it provides more clarity about which acts constitute discrimination.

4. This sample has an expansive definition of protected classes, and it includes vendors and customers within the purview of the equal opportunity policy.

5. This policy takes a more proactive stance on nondiscrimination, explains what the organization is committed to doing, and provides a reporting procedure for those who want clarification or redress.

SUGGESTED RESOURCES

- Gordon, Jack. *Pfeiffer's Classic Activities for Diversity Training.* New York: Pfeiffer, 2005.

- Ober|Kaler, attorneys at law. *The Nonprofit Legal Landscape.* Washington, DC: BoardSource, 2005.

- Society for Human Resource Management: www.shrm.org

- The U.S. Equal Employment Opportunity Commission: www.eeoc.gov/facts/ qanda.html

3. NEPOTISM

INTRODUCTION

Nepotism is a conflict-of-interest issue involving favoritism shown to relatives or friends or, more specifically, to the employment of relatives and the supervision of one relative by another. Usually nepotism refers to employment practices, but it also has board implications. The simple fact of having family members or spouses reporting to each other or serving on the same board raises questions concerning accountability, conflicts of interest (see Part 1: Ethics and Accountability, Section 4: Conflict of Interest) and independent-mindedness. At the staff level, it may also foster resentment among colleagues.

KEY ELEMENTS

- Nepotism policies should define what the organization means by nepotism, specify who is a relative, and make clear what employment relationships are prohibited.

- A nepotism policy can reduce the likelihood of questionable practices and perceptions by providing the chief executive with a routine way to avoid pressures to hire individuals based on their relationship with someone close to the organization rather than on needed skills.

PRACTICAL TIPS

✓ Consider extending the definition of a family member to include "significant others" (who should be clearly defined) and close friends.

✓ Especially for community-based organizations, it may help to illustrate examples, such as the major donor's daughter who can build the Web site for only $250, the staff member trying to find summer work for his college-age son, the board member's cousin who promises to do the job cheaply, or the employee's friend looking for a career change.

SAMPLE NEPOTISM POLICIES

The sample policies, while all relatively short, start with the most straightforward and include various nuances, ranging from spouses to donors.

1. This sample does not allow board members and staff members to be related.

2. This short policy starts with a justification for avoiding nepotism.

3. This policy, which stresses that supervisors may not work closely with family members, is more applicable for larger organizations with different departments.

4. This policy distinguishes between a spouse and other family members.

SUGGESTED RESOURCE

• Kurtz, Daniel L. and Sarah E. Paul. *Managing Conflicts of Interest: A Primer for Nonprofit Boards*. Washington, DC: BoardSource, 2006.

4. SEXUAL HARASSMENT

INTRODUCTION

Anti-sexual harassment policies are necessary for all employers, including nonprofit organizations. Sexual harassment is not only an infringement on personal dignity but it can create serious legal consequences for an individual and the entire organization. Every nonprofit should have a statement that reproves this kind of behavior and ensures prompt and thorough resolution.

KEY ELEMENTS

• A good policy should define sexual harassment, set forth a procedure for bringing a sexual harassment complaint, and define the responsibility of the nonprofit organization in responding to the complaint.

• The rights of both the accused and the accuser should be specified in the policy.

• The policy should also address the process for handling allegations, investigations, disciplinary actions, and retaliation.

PRACTICAL TIPS

✓ Many organizations do not consider simply having a policy sufficient. Consider providing sensitivity training and initiating discussions among staff on what constitutes harassment, providing a foundation for proper professional behavior. It is important to distinguish between discriminatory harassment and obnoxious behavior that does not target another individual because of sex.

✓ Provide managers with special training on their personal legal liability, as well as guidance on how to manage staff on either side of the situation.

SAMPLE SEXUAL HARASSMENT POLICIES

The policy statements provide clear examples of sexual harassment guidelines and procedures for taking action in a sexual harassment allegation.

1. This sample policy provides brief definitions of what constitutes harassment and outlines the basic steps for addressing it. It is written to apply to any kind of harassment, though it addresses sexual harassment explicitly.

2. This policy offers more detailed definitions about what constitutes sexual harassment, and assigns responsibility for addressing it to the human resources staff.

3. This policy clearly defines sexual harassment and provides detailed steps for addressing a complaint.

4. This comprehensive sample provides a thorough outline of what constitutes harassment, what procedures to follow to address the issue, and what steps to take for any necessary disciplinary action.

SUGGESTED RESOURCES

- Ober|Kaler, attorneys at law. *The Nonprofit Legal Landscape*. Washington, DC: BoardSource, 2005.

- The U.S. Equal Employment Opportunity Commission: www.eeoc.gov/facts/ fs-sex.html

5. WORKPLACE ENVIRONMENT

INTRODUCTION

A safe, congenial, and considerate work environment increases efficiency and team-work. Staff must be able to come to work feeling comfortable about collaborating and communicating with colleagues in a professional setting. Policies and guidelines protect employees and their time, as well as the organization's resources. Such policies can help create an environment with greater safety, productivity, and employee morale. The policies in this section — substance abuse, solicitation, and electronic communication — address some of the more common workplace issues that have significant ramifications for the organization.

KEY ELEMENTS

- Substance Abuse: Alcohol and illegal drugs have no place in the work environment. A substance abuse policy should define what activities are prohibited in the facility and during delivery of services. Especially for organizations that host special events, the policy should address any exceptions, such as moderate alcohol consumption at certain types of organization-sanctioned events. The policy should also outline procedures for investigating reported violations, drug testing, and due process for employees to defend themselves. Lastly, it should outline disciplinary actions, which may include referral for assistance and/or termination.

- Solicitation: Workplace solicitations — from school fundraisers to local business advertising — have the potential to get unwieldy and unfair without thoughtful policies. A clear policy on solicitation creates parameters for what is acceptable and what is inappropriate within the office setting. It should indicate who is covered (employees and/or non-employees), types of solicitation (e.g., political campaigns, commercial promotions, charitable fundraising), and restrictions (what activities are prohibited and allowed and, if allowed, under what circumstances).

- Electronic Communication: Technology is an essential communications tool in today's workplace, and its applications — such as voicemail, e-mail, and the Internet — are owned by the organization. A policy should set clear guidelines and limits for personal communication, with the understanding that occasional communication during office hours is inevitable. Organizations often reserve the right to monitor messages and Internet usage. They may also use the policy to remind employees that no means of electronic communication is fully confidential and discretion is necessary.

PRACTICAL TIPS

- ✓ The terminology used for policies ranges from substance abuse to drug-free workplace policies, and the level of specificity is likely to depend on the organization's scope of programs and services. Some organizations — such as those working with children, the elderly, or substance abusers — need more stringent prohibitions and explicit guidelines to protect their employees and their clients.

- ✓ An effective substance abuse policy is based on the organization's values. Some organizations follow a legal model that focuses on detecting and disciplining those who violate the policy. Others prefer a policy that emphasizes performance and offers assistance to those struggling with substance abuse problems.

- ✓ Discuss the solicitation policy and rationale behind it during a staff meeting. While most offices are accustomed to fundraising efforts from co-workers — on behalf of their children for Girl Scout cookies and high school raffles or on their own behalf for marathons and special events — workplace solicitations can be uncomfortable for staff who feel pressured by their supervisors, cannot afford to support their colleagues, or disagree with the cause. On the other hand, personal solicitations — properly conducted — may provide an opportunity to help someone in need or contribute to a cause.

✓ Provide bulletin boards or designate break rooms for personal announcements in order to better control and monitor office solicitations.

✓ Remind employees that the organization owns the communications systems and expects employees to use these systems to carry out their jobs. While acknowledging that individuals need to carry out certain personal business during office hours, the policy may articulate that the organization expects employees to use their lunch hour and break time for such personal business.

✓ Change all systems passwords regularly as an added protective device.

SAMPLE WORKPLACE ENVIRONMENT POLICIES

The eight policies included address the above-defined subcategories: substance abuse, office solicitation, and electronic communication.

1. This policy, with emphasis on working with minors, provides stringent prohibitions against alcohol and drugs, as well as cigarettes, within the office environment.

2. This policy frames the restrictions for substance use in terms of the workplace environment, allows moderate alcohol consumption during work-related events, and calls for drug testing when necessary.

3. This sample provides detailed guidance for handling the service of alcohol during events.

4. This policy elaborates on the use of drugs and alcohol and includes more specific guidelines about drug testing.

5. This policy generally prohibits solicitations in the office space, except when approved by management or otherwise allowed by law.

6. This policy frames solicitation issues in terms of work disruptions and generally prohibits any solicitations, with the exception of recognized charities.

7. This policy limits electronic communication to legitimate business purposes.

8. This sample provides clear guidelines for e-mail and Internet use, as well as personal telephone calls during business hours.

SUGGESTED RESOURCES

• Ober|Kaler, attorneys at law. *The Nonprofit Legal Landscape.* Washington, DC: BoardSource, 2005.

• Society for Human Resource Management: www.shrm.org

• U.S. Department of Health and Human Services: http://workplace.samhsa.gov/ WPWorkit/safety.html#intro

6. COMPLAINTS

INTRODUCTION

For some organizations, the board of directors may act as the court of last resort for complaints that cannot be solved at the staff level. While it is generally the chief executive's responsibility to hear staff complaints, a responsible board, in order to avoid costly lawsuits or adverse publicity, may want to try to resolve a dispute before it goes outside of the organization. In order to avoid undermining the authority of the chief executive, the board should provide guidance on the specific kinds of cases it will deal with, such as accusations of improper conduct against the chief executive. The board should therefore make sure its complaint procedure policy is up to date and is being implemented by management.

KEY ELEMENTS

- Standard and clear policies that are consistently enforced are the primary prevention against employee complaints. Equitable and fair treatment of employees should be the rule for supervisors.

- The policy may provide a process for the use of outside mediation when no other solution seems feasible or acceptable to both parties.

PRACTICAL TIPS

- ✓ Clarify the proper hierarchy for complaints. Unless the supervisor is the cause for a complaint, he or she should generally be the first contact.

- ✓ Indicate the role of the board in the process. Most personnel issues should remain within the purview of the chief executive and the board should not get involved. However, when the complaint is about the chief executive or management has allegedly not reacted to a serious complaint, it may be acceptable to permit staff to contact the board.

- ✓ Immediate reaction and thorough investigation are essential in handling employment complaints. Supervisors should keep a written record of every complaint.

- ✓ A complaint procedure document functions as a parallel process to whistleblower policies (see Part I: Ethics and Accountability, Section 6: Whistleblower Protection). In developing the procedure, consider its relationship to this other policy.

SAMPLE COMPLAINTS POLICIES

These samples provide alternative ways of framing complaint policies by focusing on different aspects of the resolution process.

1. This brief policy provides basic guidelines for a speedy resolution to a complaint.

2. This brief policy stresses that the board is only to be used as a court of last resort.

3. This sample outlines a process and timeline for resolving a complaint.

4. This policy outlines an informal and a formal administrative review process for handling complaints, including suggested time limits for resolving them.

5. This sample document clarifies the respective responsibilities of those involved in addressing a complaint.

SUGGESTED RESOURCES

- American Bar Association Coordinating Committee. *Guide to Nonprofit Corporate Governance in the Wake of Sarbanes-Oxley*. Chicago, IL: American Bar Association, 2005.

- Ober|Kaler, attorneys at law. *The Nonprofit Legal Landscape*. Washington, DC: BoardSource, 2005.

- *Taking the High Road: A Guide to Effective and Legal Employment Practices for Nonprofits*. Washington, DC: The Nonprofit Risk Management Center, 1999.

7. PERFORMANCE REVIEW

INTRODUCTION

Even if the board is not involved in evaluating the performance of staff, other than the chief executive, it is valuable to have organizational policies in place that stress the importance of these assessments. The purpose of annual performance evaluation is to clarify goals and ensure that they are met, foster communication between an employee and the supervisor, and identify areas that benefit from professional development.

KEY ELEMENTS

- It should be clear who is involved in the assessment process, how, and when.

- Written records of the process and results should be kept, no matter how informal the process is.

- All employees should understand how the evaluation results are used in setting compensation and sharing potential bonuses.

PRACTICAL TIPS

✓ Create a standard form for the employee's self-assessment and another one for the use of the supervisor. Evaluate the effectiveness of these forms from time to time.

✓ Require all employees to review their job descriptions annually to ensure that they are still accurate.

✓ Ensure that there is a meeting between the employee and the supervisor to discuss any discrepancies in the evaluation and/or steps to take to implement recommendations.

SAMPLE PERFORMANCE REVIEW POLICIES

The sample policies provide the basis for performance evaluation by stating that there is a process in place, how to deal with performance that does not meet expectations, and how the evaluation results relate to compensation.

1. This short policy simply states that performance evaluation takes place annually.

2. This policy focuses on the relationship between performance evaluation and compensation.

3. This policy outlines the disciplinary courses of action for unsatisfactory performance or unprofessional conduct. While not a complaint policy, it follows similar steps and processes for dealing with a difficult situation.

SUGGESTED RESOURCES

• Center for Organization Effectiveness: www.greatorganizations.com

• Mintz, Joshua and Jane Pierson. *Assessment of the Chief Executive, Revised.* Washington, DC: BoardSource, 2005.

• Pynes, Joan E. *Human Resources Management for Public and Nonprofit Organizations, 2nd Edition.* San Francisco: Jossey-Bass, 2004.

Part VII: Communications

1. Media Relations

Introduction

Organizations can get into public relations trouble if too many people attempt to speak to the media on behalf of the organization, especially in emergency situations. An organizational media policy should include the development of positive, consistent messages; print and other supporting documents (including a one-page description of the organization and a press kit); and a pool of official spokespeople versed on issues that are important to the organization. By having a media policy and establishing a designated media contact — whether an officer or a staff member — the organization can help to avoid potential story inaccuracies, conflicting messages, and/or press leaks. And, in the event that the story relates to improper actions by the chief executive or members of the board, the board may want to elect an impartial spokesperson to act as the principal media contact.

Key Elements

- The rationale behind a media policy is to ensure consistency of message. Therefore, the policy should clearly state who may speak on behalf of the organization. For some nonprofits, such as those that work on public policy issues, the media policy may designate subject matter experts on staff who have more latitude in speaking with the media on certain issues.

- The media policy needs to establish the chain of command for handling media inquiries and clarify the communication process. It should also include alternatives if the primary spokesperson is not available or if the inquiry relates to that individual.

- The policy should provide direction on whether (and what) documents may be shared with the media. All media relations should be consistent with and supportive of the overall communications objectives of the organization.

- The policy emphasizes that, as a general rule of thumb, individual board members (other than the board chair) are normally not authorized spokespersons for an organization. Instead, the board chair, the chief executive, or another designated representative should speak for the organization.

Practical Tips

- ✓ In sharing the media policy with board and staff, explain why it is important to have a single contact person (or a designated group) for all media inquiries.

- ✓ This designated spokesperson must be able to communicate with a reporter, even if he or she needs to rely on others to provide talking points or to designate someone else to handle technical information. When appropriate, the designated spokesperson may have other staff members provide additional information to the reporter.

✓ Develop and share documents that contain basic organizational talking points that board and staff members can use to introduce the organization and its activities.

✓ If any media inquiry involves an allegation of wrongdoing by the organization or any of its officers, directors, or employees, engage the organization's legal counsel prior to any statements being made to the media or to the general public. In some instances, an individual accused of wrongdoing may need to retain his or her own legal counsel and may not be able to communicate with the organization's legal counsel in order to avoid waiving the attorney-client privilege.

SAMPLE MEDIA RELATIONS POLICIES

General media policies tend to be brief, with more specific guidelines included in procedures. The samples provided include general media policies and a media procedures document.

1. This short policy is for a small organization that is concerned about consistency of the message.

2. This brief policy provides additional guidelines, such as including the board president as an authorized spokesperson and requiring advance approval from the chief executive.

3. This succinct policy allows the chief executive to speak out on public policy issues on behalf of the organization.

4. This statement outlines the procedures for anyone responding to a media inquiry and serves as a useful complement to the basic policy.

5. This policy, tailored to federated organizations, guides chapters to share media attention with the national office.

SUGGESTED RESOURCES

- Feinglass, Art. *The Public Relations Handbook for Nonprofits: A Comprehensive and Practical Guide*. San Francisco: Jossey-Bass, 2005.

- Lukas, Carol and Linda Hoskins. *Nonprofit Guide to Conducting Community Forums: Engaging Citizens, Mobilizing Communities*. St. Paul, MN: Fieldstone Alliance, 2003.

- Patterson, Sally J. *Generating Buzz: Strategic Communications for Nonprofit Boards*. Washington, DC: BoardSource, 2006.

- Wymer, Walter W, ed. *Journal of Nonprofit & Public Sector Marketing*. Binghamton, NY: The Haworth Press.

2. CRISIS COMMUNICATIONS

INTRODUCTION

In every organization there is the possibility of a crisis, internal or external. The nature of that crisis, its origin, and its potential impact will determine how the organization responds. Potential crises should be identified *before* they happen, with overall processes to set in motion when necessary. These processes naturally need to be fine-tuned and finalized when actually faced with the real thing.

Nonprofits generally deal with two kinds of crises: emergencies and controversies. Emergencies are unpredictable events that wreak havoc on the organization and those it serves; they include everything from thefts and accidents to fires and tornadoes. Controversies are crises that threaten the organization's reputation, such as accusations of fraud, legal disputes, or leadership conflicts. Regardless of the situation, a crisis communication policy is intended to help the board and staff act swiftly and consistently under stressful circumstances.

KEY ELEMENTS

- The process for communicating with media and the general public should be defined. Addressing the different kinds of crises your organization may be faced with and providing guidelines for how to deal with them is essential.

- The crisis team, the key spokespersons, and the chain of command should be identified through a telephone tree or other immediate communication mechanism, with authority levels and supervisory roles clarified. In a crisis situation, accountability is important in order to avoid mixed messages.

- Organizational priorities in the policy should be set during a crisis. Safety of employees and customers always comes first.

PRACTICAL TIPS

- ✓ The follow-on to a crisis communications policy is a crisis communications plan. Have a plan and follow it in order to minimize or avoid negative effects.

- ✓ Staff members shoulder the responsibility for emergencies, and they often tap the board for support and resources. The chief executive and the board should bear the burden of controversies, unless the chief executive is actually involved in the controversy.

SAMPLE CRISIS COMMUNICATIONS POLICIES

The first sample policy offers a general approach; the second provides more explicit details when faced with a crisis.

1. This general policy captures the organization's approach to media relations and contemplates an emergency situation.

2. This longer policy addresses crisis communications specifically, and it includes clear guidelines and responsibility for responding.

SUGGESTED RESOURCES

- Hobby, Frederick D. "Staying Cool under the Hot Lights." *Associations Now.* October 2005.

- Larson, Laurie. "When to Say What: Trustees and the Media." *Trustee.* May 2002.

- Patterson, Sally J. *Generating Buzz: Strategic Communications for Nonprofit Boards.* Washington, DC: BoardSource, 2006.

3. ELECTRONIC MEDIA

INTRODUCTION

Nonprofit organizations communicate with a vast array of audiences in many different formats. Technology increases the opportunities for better communications but introduces a new set of risks related to electronic media.

Most nonprofit organizations use e-mail, have their own Web sites, and conduct commercial activities via the Internet. Accuracy of information and individual privacy are critical issues. The scope of electronic media policies seems limitless as electronic communications become the primary means of sharing information.

KEY ELEMENTS

- It is important for Web sites to offer accurate information and provide copyright clarification, and to be updated regularly.

- Policies should cover risk-management issues, such as electronic back ups, data storage, access authorities, passwords, and general office etiquette for electronic communication.

PRACTICAL TIPS

- ✓ On your Web site, make sure visitors know what to expect when using your materials or engaging in a transaction — both to protect the organization's intellectual capital and ensure their privacy.

- ✓ Don't make promises you can't keep. State carefully what information is shared and what is not shared with outsiders. For instance, if your organization accepts credit card payments via the Web site and your fulfillment is handled by a third party, you inevitably share this information as part of completing the transaction.

- ✓ Have your IT team regularly communicate with staff to remind them of the expected procedures for everyone.

These sample policies address multiple issues, from updating electronic information, to privacy, to public access to online services. They are designed only as a sampling of the different aspects of electronic media that might warrant policies.

1. This brief policy statement provides guidelines for updating electronic documents and records that the organization uses to communicate with its constituents.

2. This privacy policy sets parameters for use of electronic data collected through the Internet.

SUGGESTED RESOURCES

- Hart, Ted, James M. Greenfield, and Michael Johnston. *Nonprofit Internet Strategies: Best Practices for Marketing, Communications, and Fundraising Success.* New York: John Wiley & Sons, 2005.

- Hopkins, Bruce R. *The Nonprofits' Guide to Internet Communications Law.* New York: John Wiley & Sons, 2002.

4. LOBBYING AND POLITICAL ACTIVITY

INTRODUCTION

Nonprofit organizations frequently want to — and do — engage in political activities, but federal tax laws regulate what is permissible. The restrictions are very important because the penalties for violating them are serious, from taxes to fines, and even revocation of tax exemption. Federal law defines actions designed to influence or affect legislation as lobbying, and actions designed to affect elections as electioneering.

The nature of an organization's tax exemption shapes what it may and may not do. For example, public charities (501(c)(3)s) may engage in lobbying, within limits, but not electioneering. Yet, they may conduct voter education and get-out-the-vote efforts, which are not considered electioneering. In contrast, social welfare organizations (501(c)(4)s) and trade associations (501(c)(6)s) have more latitude with both lobbying and electioneering. Private foundations, on the other hand, may not earmark *any* part of their grants for lobbying purposes. Nor may organizations use federal grant funds for lobbying activities.

KEY ELEMENTS

- Even though the law is strict about lobbying by public charities, a policy not only spells out what is acceptable within your organization but also reminds people of what is prohibited.

- It is not uncommon to find two related but independent entities. Charities that deal with public policy issues, such as children's welfare, environmental protection, or human rights, may create a social welfare organization to separate lobbying and advocacy work from educational and service delivery activities. Likewise, trade associations and professional societies may create foundations so they can receive charitable contributions for scholarships and other educational programs. It is important that the distinction between the two organizations is clear in their structure (boards, bookkeeping, etc.) as well as their messaging.

- If a public charity engages in lobbying, it should distinguish grass-roots from direct lobbying. Grass-roots lobbying includes activities designed to influence legislation by encouraging the general public, or a segment of it, to contact legislators. Direct lobbying includes communicating directly with legislators involved in formulating the legislation.

PRACTICAL TIPS

✓ Within the organization, clarify who is responsible for lobbying activities and how the funds will be tracked. The latter, in particular, has implications for the organization's overall reporting requirements.

✓ Federal tax law allows 501(c)(3) public charities to engage in lobbying within certain limits. An organization may choose one of two tests when determining the extent of its lobbying activities: 1) the "no substantial part" test, which the IRS does not define explicitly; and 2) the expenditures test, also known as the 501(h) election, which sets specific dollar limits based on the organization's total expenses.

✓ Before embarking on lobbying activities (under a 501(h) election), a charity should be sure that it is administratively equipped to handle the significant record keeping required. For example, it must be able to track staff time and expenses not only for communicating with legislators but also for preparing for the contact, conducting the research, and writing the communications. Additionally, it must document all direct costs, such as printing and mailing, related to lobbying activities.

✓ Because the definitions of legislative activity can be murky and because of the many exceptions and exemptions, those nonprofit organizations that are involved in any kind of legislative activity should seek guidance from legal counsel. The risks are too great should the organization make a mistake.

SAMPLE LOBBYING AND POLITICAL ACTIVITY POLICIES

The samples introduce a range of issues, including definitions, limitations, and acceptable practices.

1. This policy outlines the parameters for limited lobbying, reporting requirements, and clarifies what constitutes lobbying. It also provides guidance to field offices of the organization.

2. This brief policy statement is strict about inappropriate political contributions.

3. This more complicated policy, from an organization that focuses on public policy issues, outlines what employees may and may not do during elections.

SUGGESTED RESOURCES

- Pidgeon, Jr., Walter P. (Editor). *The Legislative Labyrinth: A Map for Not-for-Profits*. New York: John Wiley & Sons, 2001.

- Sen, Rinku and Kim Klein (Series Editor). *Stir It Up: Lessons in Community Organizing and Advocacy*. San Francisco: Jossey-Bass, 2003.

- *The Connection: Strategies for Creating and Operating 501(c)(3)s, 501(c)(4)s, and Political Organizations*. Washington, DC: Alliance for Justice, 2006.

Part VIII: Committees

Overview of Committees

1. Governance Committee

2. Financial Committees (Finance, Audit, and Investment)

3. Development Committee

4. Executive Committee

5. Other Common Committees

6. Advisory Councils

7. Committee Chair Job Descriptions

Overview of Committees

Committees are often considered the workhorses of the board because they do the majority of the board's work between meetings, thereby allowing the full board to focus on the big picture and critical decisions. Committee work engages board members in regular activities that extend their responsibilities far beyond participation in board meetings. Committees allow the organization to tap into an individual board member's full experience, talents, interests, and enthusiasm. They can also expand the board member's understanding of the organization, and they are often the training ground for prospective board members and future board officers.

The full board determines which committees or task forces are necessary and the general purpose of each committee. Committee structure should flow from the organization's strategic goals and the board's priorities. Periodically, the board should review its committee structure and determine which committees are necessary. Nonprofit boards are moving toward using fewer standing committees and more short-term task forces (or ad hoc committees).

The easiest way to keep the committee structure simple and flexible is to limit the number of standing committees to the bare minimum and to supplement these with a few less permanent work groups (e.g., ad hoc committees, task forces, advisory councils) to deal with specific short-term assignments such as an executive search, strategic planning, or a special event. No matter how many committees it needs, the board should always make sure each committee has a significant amount of ongoing and important work to do. If a committee does not have ongoing work, it should be disbanded.

Board committees often fail when they do not know what they are supposed to do. Therefore, giving them definite areas of responsibility, or charges, is crucial for their successful functioning. While bylaws may state the roles of particular standing committees, separate committee charters should define their specific responsibilities. Remember, the board determines the charter for the committee, not the committee itself.

A guiding statement about committees may articulate how committee chairs are selected and who may serve on each committee. Often, the board chair appoints committee chairs from the board. The role of the committee chair should always be defined (see Part VIII: Committees, Section 7: Committee Chair Job Descriptions). The chair of the committee runs the committee process and leads the work group to accomplish the expected tasks. Committee members may be board members or other interested individuals, and they may be appointed by the board chair or by the committee chair.

Sample Board Committees Protocol

While every committee has its own purpose, style, and structure, a set of standards offers the board guidelines for creating and using committees effectively. The following protocol serves as a starting point for each organization to determine what is appropriate for its committees.

1. The board will decide what committees will be formed and appoint a board member to chair each committee.

2. Non-board members can be invited to be part of the committee.

3. The committee chair is authorized to approach prospective committee members based on the prior approval of the board chair.

4. A committee meeting can be called by the chair of the committee or by the chair of the full board.

5. Each committee will be made up of a minimum of three and maximum of eight members approved by the board chair. A majority of the committee members shall constitute a quorum for any decision of the committee.

6. The board will set the goals of the committee, while the committee will set its own strategies for reaching those goals.

7. Prior to the first meeting of the committee, the board chair, the chief executive, and the committee chair will meet to review the goals and expectations set by the board and this protocol.

8. Committees will meet at least every other month, alternating with full board meetings. The chair of the committee will report in writing at the following board meeting the progress and activities of the committee.

9. The board chair and the chief executive can sit on any committee *ex officio*. They will be copied on all committee correspondence.

10. Staff persons present at a committee meeting will be present to assist because of knowledge of the actual day-to-day operations. An important job of the head of the committee is to protect the staff from being assigned tasks inappropriate to the committee.

11. The chief executive is responsible for communicating to staff members their role in committee deliberations.

12. A committee will not enter into any contractual obligations on behalf of the board.

1. GOVERNANCE COMMITTEE

INTRODUCTION

A growing trend among nonprofit boards is the establishment of a governance committee that deals with a range of issues around board development and performance. This committee is often responsible for assessing the board's current composition and identifying needs, developing board member and officer job descriptions, creating a recruitment plan and timeline, identifying and cultivating prospective members, and coordinating officer elections. In addition, the governance committee may be responsible for broader board management issues, such as reviewing board policies, board self-assessment, and a board action plan.

KEY ELEMENTS

- The committee's role as the coordinating group for overall board performance should be defined in the committee charter or job description.

- In the committee charter or job description, the committee's coordinating role in board recruitment and, as appropriate, board policies and procedures related to composition should be articulated. For example, many organizations clarify whether board members (and officers) are elected individually or as a slate. Others provide authority for this committee to handle difficult issues related to individual board member performance.

- Other aspects of board education that fall into the governance committee's purview should be included, such as officer job descriptions, orientation, educational items on board meeting agendas, and board retreats.

- The committee may also be charged with addressing board structure and performance, such as reviewing the current committee structure, leading the board self-assessment process, and updating bylaws.

PRACTICAL TIPS

- ✓ The governance committee is the board's mechanism for looking after itself. As such, its work is vital to the health of the board and the entire organization. It should ensure that the board is doing its job to provide leadership and oversight to the organization and that individual board members are carrying out their duties (see also Part II: Board and Board Members, Section 1: Role of the Board).

- ✓ This committee has evolved from the traditional nominating committee and is sometimes known as the board development committee or committee on trustees. Consider framing it as a governance committee, rather than a nominating committee, in order to address the need to consider recruitment as one critical step in a larger board building process.

- ✓ Many governance committees have the difficult task of deciding how to handle the poor performance of individual board members. This will occur naturally when their terms come up, and it may also happen along the way. Because these are often sensitive issues, they are best handled in this kind of smaller work group setting and with active involvement by the board chair and chief executive.

SAMPLE GOVERNANCE COMMITTEE JOB DESCRIPTIONS

The sample governance committee descriptions range from short and general to more comprehensive and explicit.

1. This short sample clearly defines the committee's purpose as recruiting and educating board members.

2. This sample articulates the general committee purpose and outlines the recruitment process.

3. This charter defines the composition of the committee and assigns the committee responsibility for reviewing individual board member performance.

4. This more comprehensive job description outlines five areas of responsibility related to board effectiveness.

SUGGESTED RESOURCES

- Hughes, Sandra R. "Governing More, Nominating Less." *Foundation News & Commentary*. January/February 2003.

- Hughes, Sandra R., Berit M. Lakey, and Marla J. Bobowick. *The Board Building Cycle: Nine Steps to Finding, Recruiting, and Engaging Nonprofit Board Members.* Washington, DC: BoardSource, 2000.

- Lakey, Berit M., Sandra R. Hughes, and Outi Flynn. *Governance Committee.* Washington, DC: BoardSource, 2004.

2. FINANCIAL COMMITTEES (FINANCE, AUDIT, AND INVESTMENT)

INTRODUCTION

The financial committees of a nonprofit organization are truly at the heart of the public's trust. The full board has the ultimate responsibility for and fiduciary obligation to the organization; it also has the authority to delegate specific tasks to a single or multiple financial committees. Common financial committees include finance committees, audit committees, and investment committees. The appropriate committee structure depends on several factors, including organizational size, financial complexity, sources of income, and regulatory oversight.

KEY ELEMENTS

- Finance Committee: The finance committee is responsible for monitoring the organization's overall financial health. Its core duties include overseeing budgeting and financial planning, safeguarding the organization's assets and reviewing its insurance coverage, reviewing and proposing internal controls and fiscal policies, anticipating financial problems, and ensuring that the board receives accurate and timely financial reports (see also Part IV: Finance and Investments.)

- Audit Committee: When feasible, a separate audit committee provides a nonprofit with better checks and balances. The audit committee's principal responsibilities are to hire an independent auditor, review the audit report with the auditor, and ensure that appropriate internal controls are in place. This is not a policy-making body; rather, its role is to help the board carry out its fiduciary duties (see also Part IV: Finance and Investments, Section 6: Financial Audits).

- Investment Committee: For nonprofits with considerable reserves, a separate investment committee offers additional guidance and oversight of the organization's assets. The committee's purpose is not to provide professional investment advice and services, but to establish guidelines, hire and evaluate professional advisors, and monitor investment performance (see also Part IV: Finance and Investments, Section 4: Investments and Section 5: Reserves and Endowments).

PRACTICAL TIPS

✓ When recruiting board members, keep in mind the need for financial proficiency. Not every board member needs to be a financial expert, but each board needs some members with specialized skills and knowledge — such as accounting, taxes, investing, and financial planning — to guide the board's oversight and to communicate complicated financial issues to the rest of the board.

✓ Particularly in the beginning of an organization's lifecycle, one committee may be responsible for all financial oversight. As the nonprofit's fiscal activities become more complicated, consider creating separate committees. These specialized committees often require more professional expertise and technical skills from board members.

✓ For those organizations with a single financial committee, be sure committee members understand when they are wearing the budget, financial oversight, investment, and audit hats.

✓ In the wake of the Sarbanes-Oxley Act of 2002, some state laws require that organizations with certain budget levels have a separate audit committee with independent and financially literate members. Whether the audit committee is established as a standing committee or on an ad hoc basis, it is recommended that its membership be different from that of the finance committee. (See Part I: Ethics and Accountability for information about other Sarbanes-Oxley-related policies; also see Part IV: Finance and Investments for sample policies related to fiscal oversight.)

✓ When an organization has accumulated sizable reserves, manages a significant planned giving program, or has an endowment, create a separate investment committee. For organizations with limited investments, investment oversight is often part of the finance committee's charge.

SAMPLE FINANCIAL COMMITTEE JOB DESCRIPTIONS

The job descriptions included — except for the first two — separate the finance, audit, and investment committees and include a range from brief to more specific duties of the different committees.

1. This all-purpose list of finance committee responsibilities, especially appropriate for a small organization without staff, includes budgeting, financial reporting, the audit, and investment management.

2. This committee job description provides a basic framework for a combined finance and audit committee.

3. This short job description separates basic financial oversight duties from audit and investment responsibilities.

4. This more comprehensive job description defines the role of the finance committee in terms of planning and oversight. Note that it does not involve the board in managing the finances on a daily basis.

5. This short committee job description, which assumes a separate audit committee, outlines specific duties of the committee in hiring and working with the auditor.

6. This job description provides a more specific list of responsibilities for a separate audit committee.

7. This thorough committee charter describes the role and structure of the audit committee in great detail. It is most suitable for organizations with complex financial systems, revenues from multiple sources, and/or numerous funds to manage.

8. This job description lists the basic responsibilities of a separate investment committee.

9. This concise job description assigns the monitoring and reporting of investments to a separate investment committee and acknowledges the role of outside investment professionals.

SUGGESTED RESOURCES

- Boutin, Christopher C. "Responding to Governance Challenges: The Audit Committee." *Trustee.* April 2003.

- Fry, Robert P. *Minding the Money: An Investment Guide for Nonprofit Board Members.* Washington, DC: BoardSource, 2004.

- McLaughlin, Thomas A. *Financial Committees.* Washington, DC: BoardSource, 2004.

- Ruppel, Warren. *Not-for-Profit Audit Committee Best Practices.* New York: John Wiley & Sons, 2006.

3. Development Committee

Introduction

The development committee is often charged with planning and implementing the organization's fundraising program in concert with the professional staff. The development committee follows the basic premise of other board committees: to establish policies for decision making, to engage the board in developing strategy, and to monitor implementation. In addition, development committees often get involved directly in implementation — in this case, making personal contributions, soliciting funds, opening doors to other potential individual and institutional donors, and coordinating special events.

Key Elements

- Nonprofit organizations often have a preferred term for development — from resource development to fundraising to advancement — that reflects nuances in their approach to activities that generate non-fee-for-service income for the organization.

- A development committee ensures that appropriate fundraising policies (see also Part V: Fundraising) exist and defines the role of individual board members in fundraising. Some development committees may also undertake the task of training fellow board members on the essentials of fundraising.

- Some individual and institutional donors are most effectively cultivated by a peer or professional contact. The development committee can often gain access or initiate contact more readily than staff to such prospective donors.

- The development committee (and in turn, board members) work closely with staff. Committee composition may include non-board members, ranging from staff to volunteers. Regardless, all board members should be directly involved in fundraising (see Part V: Fundraising, Section 1: Board Member Fundraising for more information on the board's role in fundraising).

Practical Tips

- ✓ The organization's mix of income sources and its development plan should guide the board in determining if it needs a development committee and, if so, the scope of its activities and who should be involved in them.

- ✓ Because fundraising is an organizationwide effort that requires board leadership, staff planning and execution, and considerable volunteer effort, be sure to clarify whether the development committee is a board-level committee or an organizationwide committee (or both).

- ✓ Depending on the scope of the organization's fundraising program, consider forming subcommittees that are responsible for the various kinds of activities appropriate for the organization, such as capital campaigns, special events, or planned giving.

SAMPLE DEVELOPMENT COMMITTEE JOB DESCRIPTIONS

Development committees, in particular, need clear charges that are customized to an organization's circumstances. The sample committee job descriptions, while all relatively straightforward, provide for a range of different ways for the board to delegate responsibility for fundraising oversight and implementation.

1. This charge to the development committee provides a broad framework for board oversight and involvement in fundraising activities.

2. This job description frames the committee's work as engaging individual board members in fundraising activities at different levels.

3. This committee job description establishes two development committees. The first committee, comprised of board members only, focuses on fundraising policies and board member participation in fundraising activities. The second committee, which is not accountable to or representative of the board, enlists other stakeholders in fundraising.

4. This list of general development committee responsibilities outlines the various ways the committee provides fundraising guidance and support to the organization, the board, and staff.

5. This list addresses the development committee's responsibilities for a particular type of fundraising — major gifts — and it serves as a model for clarifying committee and/or board responsibilities for other specific types of fundraising activities.

6. This committee charge addresses some of the unique resource development issues related to associations.

SUGGESTED RESOURCES

- Irwin-Wells, Suzanne. *Planning and Implementing Your Major Gifts Campaign.* San Francisco: Jossey-Bass, 2001.

- Lysakowski, Linda. *Nonprofit Essentials: Recruiting and Training Fundraising Volunteers.* New York: John Wiley & Sons, 2005.

- Tempel, Eugene R. *Development Committee.* Washington, DC: BoardSource, 2004.

- The Fund Raising School, Center on Philanthropy at Indiana University: www.philanthropy.iupui.edu/funds.html

4. EXECUTIVE COMMITTEE

INTRODUCTION

The structure and function of executive committees have begun to change to avoid having the executive committee as the board's "inner circle." Some executive committees are empowered only to stand in for the board and make decisions when the board cannot meet. Other executive committees have broader duties, such as policy development, evaluating the chief executive, or strategic planning. Still others have simplified their responsibilities to dealing only with emergency concerns and issues that pertain to the employment and performance of the chief executive.

Regardless of the executive committee's particular job description, it is important for the board to understand that the executive committee is not, ever, intended to take the place of the full board and that most decisions made by the executive committee should be ratified by the board. More and more boards realize that in today's world, with easy and quick e-mail and cell phone access, many urgent issues that a traditional executive committee would handle are now handled by the full board through electronic communication and ratification at the next board meeting.

KEY ELEMENTS

- Limitations on the authority of the executive committee are listed in the bylaws. Usually, an executive committee is precluded from making key organizational decisions, such as amending bylaws, removing board members, firing the chief executive, and approving major changes to the organization's structure (such as a merger).

- Executive committees are commonly used to guide and assist large boards, make decisions for the board in the case of an emergency, help coordinate the work of a board with a complicated committee structure, assist work of a geographically dispersed board, and facilitate the chief executive's access to the board.

- The job description should establish who is on the executive committee. Often it is comprised of board officers, committee chairs, and sometimes a few other "at large" board members.

- The job description should define the true purpose of the executive committee. It should also clearly define the circumstances that constitute an unmitigated emergency and when the board is unable or has no need to convene. The purpose of this clarification is to eliminate decisions that the committee makes when an issue is better handled by the full board.

- If the executive committee is responsible for certain board leadership tasks, they should be clearly defined. The ability of the executive committee to act on behalf of the organization without full board approval should be carefully delineated. Such special tasks may include the chief executive's performance review, board self-assessment, and/or serving as the court of appeal. Note that some organizations delegate these tasks to other ad hoc or standing committees.

PRACTICAL TIPS

✓ While many boards find the committee to be useful, emerging trends in nonprofit governance lean towards the elimination of an executive committee, opting for a more informal leadership group of board officers with meetings on an as-needed basis.

✓ Each board must decide for itself whether an executive committee is the right thing. Remember, however, that the only credible reason to form an executive committee is to help the board do its job, which is to make sure the organization accomplishes its mission within a legal and ethical framework.

✓ Periodically, review the performance of the executive committee specifically to determine whether it is an asset or a liability to the organization. This determination depends upon a variety of factors, including the rationale that brought the committee about in the first place, the clarity of its duties and guidelines of conduct, its structure, and how well it keeps the board — its boss — in the loop.

SAMPLE EXECUTIVE COMMITTEE JOB DESCRIPTIONS

The sample job descriptions delegate varying degrees of authority and different kinds of activities to the executive committee.

1. This brief list allows the executive committee to act on behalf of the board in emergencies.

2. This brief sample defines the executive committee as a sounding board for the chief executive.

3. This job description, which is best suited to an organization with few other committees, delegates certain organizational oversight responsibilities to the executive committee.

4. This job description establishes the limits to the authority of the executive committee.

5. This charter provides a detailed job description defining the executive committee as supporting the board and as liaison to the chief executive.

SUGGESTED RESOURCES

- Andringa, Robert C. and Ted W. Engstrom. *Nonprofit Board Answer Book: Practical Guide for Board Members and Chief Executives*. Washington, DC: BoardSource, 2002.

- Bobowick, Marla J., Sandra R. Hughes, and Berit M. Lakey. *Transforming Board Structure: Strategies for Committees and Task Forces*. Washington, DC: BoardSource, 2001.

- Light, Mark. *Executive Committee*. Washington, DC: BoardSource, 2004.

5. OTHER COMMON COMMITTEES

INTRODUCTION

In reviewing the work needed to accomplish the organization's strategic goals and prepare for a healthy future, a board might need additional committees. Some might be standing committees, but more often these are ad hoc committees or temporary task forces. Their activities may be to carry out the board's leadership and oversight duties in specific areas, or to provide additional support and resources to the organization at more of a staff or volunteer level. Some of the common additional committees are compensation, strategic planning, and public relations. Additionally, associations often have membership committees, and foundations often have grantmaking committees.

KEY ELEMENTS

- Compensation: Boards that are too large and unwieldy to manage the compensation process as a group may delegate oversight of the chief executive's compensation to a special committee or task force. A smaller committee can devote its attention as needed to the often detailed process of managing compensation matters. Some compensation committees also review other senior staff compensation levels, set annual performance objectives with the chief executive, and facilitate the chief executive's performance review. (See also Part III: Chief Executive, Section 3: Executive Compensation.)

- Strategic Planning: Strategic planning is usually a periodic activity that requires participation by board and senior staff members. The board's role is to establish strategic direction, and the staff's role is to flesh out goals and create a plan that will guide the organization for the next several years. A strategic planning committee or task force can help ensure that the planning process is well structured, involves the right people at the right time, and integrates all aspects of the organization. Often, a temporary committee will guide the planning process through the approval stage and put mechanisms in place for the full board to monitor progress against the plan.

- Communications and Public Relations: While communications and public relations are primarily staff-driven functions, board members often get involved at two levels: oversight and direct support. Board members, because of their personal and professional relationships, can be helpful in leading and supporting outreach activities. A designated committee may help develop, implement, and oversee a public relations plan; suggest strategies for how best to communicate with media and community leaders; recommend ways to involve individual board members in communication efforts; and help the board monitor its reputation. (See also Part VII: Communications.)

- Membership: Many associations use a membership committee to engage board members in recruiting and retaining members. For associations with dedicated membership staff, a committee can help shape strategy and monitor progress for the membership program. For smaller associations with few or no staff, the board may also play an active role in defining membership criteria and benefits of membership, and recruiting new members.

- Grantmaking: Grantmaking committees are specific to private and community foundations that annually distribute part of their assets to public charities whose work the foundation elects to support. Particularly in smaller foundations with no or few staff members, these committees often consist of board members who meet on scheduled dates to select and approve recipients of funds. These committees follow overall grantmaking guidelines approved by the board and that reflect the mission of the foundation.

PRACTICAL TIPS

✓ Bylaws often define standing committees (usually governance and finance and/or audit at a minimum), but should allow for the board to create additional committees and task forces as needs arise. This flexibility helps eliminate unnecessary amendments to the bylaws when a committee is formed or disbanded, or its charter is changed.

✓ As the role of the committees is to help the board get its work done more efficiently, each board should determine carefully what committees might be necessary or practical. To avoid creating unnecessary standing committees, use ad hoc task forces to address a particular need.

SAMPLE JOB DESCRIPTIONS FOR OTHER COMMON COMMITTEES

The sample committee charters cover functions that some boards delegate to a specific standing committee or ad hoc work group (such as compensation, strategic planning, and communications), and oversight of key program areas unique to associations (membership) and foundations (grantmaking).

1. This sample states who serves on the compensation committee and gives the committee the task to evaluate the performance of the chief executive.

2. This job description outlines the overall responsibilities and structure of the compensation committee.

3. In addition to listing the overall responsibilities and structure of the compensation committee, this charter defines what constitutes total compensation.

4. This basic job description outlines the basic composition, structure, and responsibilities of the strategic planning committee.

5. This job description defines the purpose and activities of a standing strategic planning committee.

6. This sample delegates responsibility for providing guidance to and oversight of the organization's communications activities to a committee of the board.

7. This sample is an association public relations committee job description where committee members are association members and the committee reports to the board.

8. This job description establishes a board committee that is responsible for monitoring public policy and relations with stakeholders.

9. This charter outlines responsibilities of a membership committee for an association that has a national board and local chapters. Note that members of the committee need not be members of the board.

10. This association committee charter defines what the membership committee will do and how. Note that members of the committee need not be members of the board, except for a designated board liaison.

11. This sample gives the membership committee an active role in assessing the value of services provided to members, and recommending elimination or addition of member benefits.

12. This grantmaking committee charter for a community foundation clarifies the responsibilities of committee members and addresses conflict-of-interest issues.

13. These grantmaking committee expectations provide guidelines for committee members to carefully and objectively review grant applications.

SUGGESTED RESOURCES

- Association of Small Foundations: www.smallfoundations.org

- Bobowick, Marla J., Sandra R. Hughes, and Berit M. Lakey. *Transforming Board Structure: Strategies for Committees and Task Forces*. Washington, DC: BoardSource, 2001.

- Council on Foundations: www.cof.org

- Deale, Charles W.L. "The Board's Vital Role in Membership Development." *Association Management*. January 2000.

- Feinglass, Art. *The Public Relations Handbook for Nonprofits: A Comprehensive and Practical Guide*. San Francisco: Jossey-Bass, 2005.

- Karlson, David and Donald Ethier. *Association Membership Basics: A Workbook for Directors and Members*. Washington, DC: ASAE, 1997.

- Kocsis, Deborah L. and Susan A. Waechter. *Driving Strategic Planning: A Nonprofit Executive's Guide*. Washington, DC: BoardSource, 2003.

- Patterson, Sally J. *Generating Buzz: Strategic Communications for Nonprofit Boards*. Washington, DC: BoardSource, 2006.

- Peregrine, Michael W., Ralph E. DeJong, and Timothy J. Cotter. "Avoiding Scandal: Recommended Practices for Board Executive Compensation Committees." *Trustee*. July/August 2004.

- Rhoads, Paul K. *Managing a Private Foundation: Maintaining the Donor's Intent.* Washington, DC: The Philanthropy Roundtable, 1999.

- Romweber, Jane, Robbi Fox, and Michael Powers. "Compensation Committees That Work." *Directors & Boards.* Winter 2003.

6. ADVISORY COUNCILS

INTRODUCTION

Advisory councils are groups of volunteers typically assembled to supplement the governance activities carried out by the board or the management tasks carried out by staff. They can perform a variety of jobs — for example, assessing the need for new programs, raising the organization's profile in the community, gathering input from stakeholders to the organization, monitoring industry or community trends, conducting program evaluations — many of which are central to an organization's activities.

Advisory councils, however, can be difficult to manage well. They have a great deal of responsibility, and little authority. These groups grapple with issues that are central to the organization, yet their membership may well consist of people who have no formal connection with the nonprofit. To ensure their success, advisory councils must be formed with a purpose and with care. And, they must be formed in a way that benefits both the group and the nonprofit it serves.

KEY ELEMENTS

- Some advisory councils are ongoing bodies, while others have a limited term of existence defined by their charge. It is helpful to clarify whether the group is permanent or temporary, and if temporary, to fix the period if it can be determined in advance.

- Advisory councils are not legal bodies and cannot assume responsibility for the governance of an organization. Advisory council members normally have no legal responsibilities. They have no vested right to serve and no immunity from removal.

- A written statement of purpose helps an advisory council to identify the collective role of the group and to describe the responsibilities of individual members. The limits of authority and its role in making recommendations or carrying out specific tasks should be clearly defined.

- The council's goals should determine its membership, not the other way around. For a group that is designed to highlight a nonprofit's standing in the community, perhaps an advisory council packed with luminaries is appropriate. For a group that provides technical expertise, the credentials for membership may be quite different. It should be clear who appoints the members and whether members have term limits.

- Form must follow function — or the group will not function well. Issues like council size, composition, term limits, frequency of meetings, and meeting formats should be guided by the purpose of the council.

PRACTICAL TIPS

✓ An advisory council needs to be as large — or as small — as necessary to accomplish its task. It could be five members or 50 members. Fundraising advisory councils might be bigger because a larger size tends to increase an organization's reach. A group designed to provide technical expertise might be smaller.

✓ While advisory councils might not meet as often as governing boards, the number of meetings depends on the purpose of the group. Groups designed to promote special events might meet frequently during the height of planning. Others may meet only once a year, related to a particular event or to consider fiscal year-end reviews. Some may never meet collectively in person, but function well "virtually" or individually to bring a larger network of support to the organization.

✓ To avoid confusion over which entity has ultimate responsibility and authority, do not call an advisory council a board. Some alternative work group names include advisory committee, advisory council, auxiliary council, advisory or leadership task force, sponsors or friends of the organization.

✓ To recognize the efforts of the advisory council and enhance its validity, establish a formal relationship between it and the governing board. For example: designate a permanent advisory council member to serve as a liaison with the board, invite advisory council members to attend a particular board meeting, and/or include advisory council members in board/staff retreats and other special events.

SAMPLE ADVISORY COUNCIL JOB DESCRIPTIONS

The advisory council job descriptions begin with statements of generic purpose, and then provide more detailed examples that reflect specific purposes: professional development, community engagement, and fundraising.

1. This basic advisory council is designed to engage leaders in the community as volunteers to advance the organization's mission and goals. Although it mentions specific qualifications, the wording is easily modified to suit any type of organization.

2. This general job description establishes an advisory council for an association that wishes to engage its members in industry-specific issues.

3. This charter defines an advisory council that is designed to serve as a link between the organization and a variety of key stakeholders.

4. This statement of purpose focuses the advisory council on fundraising on behalf of the organization.

Suggested Resources

- Axelrod, Nancy R. *Advisory Councils.* Washington, DC: BoardSource, 2004.

- Ellis, Susan J. "Brain Picking: Thinking About an Advisory Committee." *The NonProfit Times.* May 1, 2001.

- Saidel, Judith R. and Alissandra M. D'Aquanni. "Expanding the Governance Construct: Functions and Contributions of Advisory Groups." www.nonprofitresearch.org/usr_doc/15897.pdf

7. Committee Chair Job Descriptions

Introduction

It is often said that if a committee has a good chair, then it is a good committee. The committee chair ensures that members have the information needed to do the job, and oversees the logistics of the committee's operation. The committee chair is responsible for linking the work of the committee back to the full board with reports to the board chair. Committee chairs are often, but not always, members of the board.

All committees have a chair. The general expectations for the committee chair position tend to be similar, regardless of the specific type of committee.

Key Elements

- Job descriptions for committee chairs often define the role as group leader of the committee and liaison with the full board.

- Depending on how structured the board is, committee chair job descriptions may outline particular expectations, such as creating an annual action plan and reporting regularly to the board.

- Form should follow function when it comes to committee chair job descriptions. Depending on the committee's purpose, the chair may fulfill different leadership functions. And, much will also be influenced by the level of staff support.

Practical Tips

✓ The committee chair is, or should be, held accountable for the committee's performance. This requires that the committee have a clear charter, specific goals, routine monitoring, and even periodic evaluation.

✓ The role of the committee chair is a pivotal one, not only for guiding the committee's work but also because committee chairs may be potential board chairs. Consider appointing someone to chair a committee to see how that person functions in a leadership position and/or to provide leadership training.

SAMPLE COMMITTEE CHAIR JOB DESCRIPTIONS

The committee chair job descriptions included range from general to specific, depending on how much latitude the committee chair has, the level of staff support, and the degree of autonomy that the board has granted the committee.

1. This succinct job description integrates the basic purpose of committees with the core duties of committee chairs.

2. This brief job description defines the general responsibilities for committee chairs in terms of guiding the committee's internal operations.

3. This sample, which assumes strong staff support, defines the committee chair's responsibilities to the organization, to the committee, and to the board.

4. This job description frames the committee chair's responsibilities in terms of strategy, coordination, facilitation, and communication.

5. This list of responsibilities outlines specific expectations of and procedures for committee chairs.

SUGGESTED RESOURCES

- Andringa, Robert C. and Ted W. Engstrom. *Nonprofit Board Answer Book: Practical Guide for Board Members and Chief Executives.* Washington, DC: BoardSource, 2002.

- Bobowick, Marla J., Sandra R. Hughes, and Berit M. Lakey. *Transforming Board Structure: Strategies for Committees and Task Forces.* Washington, DC: BoardSource, 2001.

- Dietel, William M. and Linda R. Dietel. *The Board Chair Handbook.* Washington, DC: BoardSource, 2001.

About the Authors

Barbara Lawrence began working as an independent consultant for nonprofit organizations in 2000, after a career that included senior executive positions in both the for-profit and nonprofit sectors. Her goal is to help nonprofit organizations achieve their missions through evidence-based decision making and sound planning. She brings research skills to the tasks of survey, market, case-building, and prospect research, as well as program evaluation. Her management skills in planning help organizations develop strategic, business, and fundraising plans, and learn to apply project management techniques. She strives to ensure that her clients are smarter and feel in control after her work is done.

Prior to working as a consultant, Barbara held positions as executive director of a nonprofit school for learning disabled children, senior vice president for an educational database and book publisher, and division director for a professional engineering society. As a volunteer, Barbara has served as chair of several boards, including the Alice Paul Institute, the Franklin Township Friends of the Library, and the National Federation of Abstracting and Information Services.

Starting her academic career as a chemist, with a BA from the University of Vermont and graduate work at Yale, Barbara followed a career path in managing and providing information services. Her continuing education includes the Wharton Executive Effectiveness and IBM Business Systems Planning programs. She is a graduate of the Clark Fellowship Foundation Center training in Fundraising Consulting.

Outi Flynn, director of Knowledge Center at BoardSource, has been part of the staff since 1989. For the past several years she has developed, structured, and managed the BoardSource Online Knowledge Center, one of the most highly utilized and popular services BoardSource offers. She is the author of *Meet Smarter: A Guide to Better Board Meetings* and co-author of *Governance Committee*.

Outi has created and contributed the bulk of the governance information available on BoardSource's Web site, including topic papers and frequently asked questions, and acts as the primary content reviewer for the organization's publications. Her areas of expertise cover overall sector issues, dilemmas that concern nonprofit leaders on a daily basis, and structural and procedural challenges that affect board productivity.